GRACE DIVINE JOURNEY

Eastern Spirituality in a Western World

Gurus, Yoga, Kundalini, Mantras

(And much more!)

By

Raymond Pattison

(Ex-monk: Paramhansa Ganesh Giri)

[Type here]

[Type here]

CONTENTS

[Type here]

Writing as provision of my life journey details, is
interspersed with the present place of *Being*. Thus, as I
write a piece of autobiography, I then interpret its place,
not only in the spiritual journey then, but also the
spiritual journey now

[Type here]

Preface to *Grace Divine Journey*

This book is a "compendium" of my previous three books. There is a chapter from *English-Man, Beggar-Man, Holy-Man*, (chapter 11), describing the last years of my life in India as a monk. (Up to 1976). I also write about my further spiritual & "ordinary" life journey. (Post 1976). It contains also a selection of my "spiritual teachings - revised & upgraded". Thus, it is a "bit of everything", so if you want to read only one of my books – this is it!

I write to teach.

Life is a teaching in its journey.

I write for the purpose of providing information, teaching and reflection on my own journey, with the purpose of engendering Enlightenment.

I was born in London 1947 and became a monk in India in 1966, after leaving London without any money, & spending a year on the "hippie trail". (I was *Paramahansa Ganesh Giri* in India – see Chap. 11). I returned to England in 1976 and then became a mental health professional. I had a family life after moving to New Zealand and later I spent more than 10 years in clinical teaching or education roles. Hence my predilection for teaching!

This book partially encompasses events in my post-India years briefly. I focus though on my spiritual/psychological journey through those years. None of this is meant to be as an autobiography. Rather it's leading to and providing background to teachings or writings.

It's all about Divine Grace for me!

I try not to present from an ego or lower self-perspective! My deity is *the Goddess,* in the forms that I became devotionally focused on in India. This Goddess is represented, (in plural), by *Durga, Kali, Lakshmi and Sarasvati.* (All One but separate just like us!). Also, *Tara* in Tibetan Buddhism.

My writing also discusses mental health and addictions, as I have some experience here! Over the years I engaged in extensive personal health searches both conventional and spiritual. Therefore, I have both professional and personal experience of the whole gamut of psychiatry, therapy, and psychology. (Including medicinal options). I am also able to say that I found a number of solutions for my issues, through all areas of my endeavors, spiritual and otherwise. I currently find myself to have moved past my search mode into *Practical Enlightenment* mode. And mentally stability. (My opinion only)!

Just to clarify I write about Enlightenment in terms of what we can all be, and in fact what we all are all in our Truth.

Accepting ones Divinity is part of the journey, and this is not to denigrate religions or philosophies of duality, as I still maintain both a non-dual approach and a devotional one. Religion may however forcefully want to us to bow down before *their* gods, higher powers, saviors and avatars. I myself have found benefit in many religions through considerable active participation, and I add those resources to the list of what helped.

I am Multi-Faith!
I am "multi-modal"! (Accepting scientific, psychiatric, and even atheistic viewpoints).

Can I do this? Currently free-thinking is still legal where I live and long may this state of affairs continue! Underpinning all of the journey therefore lies my years of practice and experience, and my intention to leave these writings as a resource for whoever finds them useful.

My bottom line is that I write for myself! (With a perspective that I believe it's my service to provide this as it is a directed endeavor, driven by my Deity and the Divine Cosmic Consciousness).

I am also grateful for my Guides and guides, and my Gurus.

The writings are teachings.

Where there is some autobiography its often followed by some "teaching content."

Chapter 1

In and out of India

How it began. (Very briefly)

I left home I London in 1965. I was 17 years old and had at that time been restless to wander off and explore the world for several years. The flames of rebellion burned within me. Rebellion from parents, & from the straight jacket of convention. I was not alone. This was when the pop-culture ushered in by the likes of The Beatles, and Rolling Stones, signified the birth of a youthful revolution that was to overturn the cultural norms of society of that time.

The anti-establishment flower power generation wanted to explore new dimensions of experience, to grow long hair, wear outrageous clothes, and experience the unexplored depths of the mind with L.S.D., alongside cannabis.

Influenced by my own generation, I ended up on the India trail, the Overland Trail to Kathmandu and Nepal. I preceded a mass migration, so by the time Westerners were flocking to India in in large numbers to the gurus, I had been in India for about 5 years.

I couldn't find what I wanted in England spiritually, because I didn't know about spirituality! I had no compass, no gurus, nobody to explain about the search for identity. My parents and I were on another planet! Attendance at church had been a requirement at times, but I had no interest in the church, or even knew that there was some consolation to be found there.

I did not even know what I was seeking!

What did I find?

Get with the Programme!

There are always lots of questions regarding the spiritual journey & spiritual pathways.

We often do things based on fear rather than what will give us enlightenment or realization.

Do you want to survive at least, if not thrive?

A lot of life becomes based on culture, politics, and even religious "rules", rather than based on a search for the Meaning and the Truth of all life.

In life most problematic things can be sorted to some degree.

Even major health issues like depression and addiction can be addressed through therapy, rehabilitation, and even medication.

Family and relationship issues can be resolved, or at least we can get to a point of resolution where we know what cannot be changed.

Then life becomes about acceptance and the serenity prayer begins to make sense.

Always, however the person who wishes to avoid pain also seeks pleasure in life.

Free choice will still take precedence.

So, regarding choice, we also have this concept of *karma*. We have suffering and pleasure, and success, and failure in proportion to our previous activities, and then our current activities create new karma.

This can be individual, but it can also be collective, as we also tend to fit in with the cultural norms for our particular society and country, or religion.

In some places if we do not toe the line on religious matters we can be killed or jailed for blasphemy!

To move past all the structures is necessary to find the Realization and Enlightenment that exists beyond.

Then what we get is *Knowing*, and therefore the essence of the world is perceived very differently.

Then it becomes possible to change things radically, because we are in a place of understanding where we can be active in life, but based on Spiritual Truth to guide us. This is probably when we get into deep meditation, yoga and our specific spiritual pathways.

Then it's possible to see the Divine, not as a summary of our knowledge or some outcome of prayer practice, but as what is "All and Everything".

Indeed, this can only be all or nothing.

God cannot be all of creation and not something within creation. Nothing can be excluded.

Light is required to see through the darkness though.

The teacher may be the Guru.

"Gu" stands for darkness and *"Ru"* stands for the piercer of the darkness, the bringer of light.

That is why we have teachers to bring light to our pathways until we no longer need them. We don't need to put them on a pedestal, or become fanatics, as we just need a little light so we can get on our way. Thanks very much!

What we see in the light is very different from what we see in the dark.

In the light all is somewhat ok to live with. Sure, even the bad people!

Of course, how are you achieve this "level" is up to you.

Religion of your choice or choose what you will as your pathway.

The information in this teaching is only "an example". If it has a use, take of it what you will.

By all means your way may be the only way and the only truth for you.

It's just normal human behavior to do things from free-will/choice.

However, when you are really in the Light you will not need to judge others.

Neither their spiritual practice, nor their religion, nor their culture, nor their political beliefs-ever!

You will know who you are and what the Truth is of: *Life and the Universe*, and that the world around you, are an emanation of the Divine in its entirety.

You will then really understand what your purpose is and what the human body is all about.

However, if you deny some part of your life you won't be able to see the fullness of the Divine Energy, and part of you stays in darkness.

This goes down to the level of service, and how you treat your fellow human beings. How you deal with the homeless, the sick and the mentally unwell.

This is not about being like Jesus or the Buddha. You don't have to like anyone particularly. You don't have to make friends with everyone. But you do need to recognize the Divine in all, and in all people.

This way of being has always been present, and the great sages and seers, and incarnations have been on earth to help us to see the pathways, and sometimes to push us gently, (or a lot).

Nature sometimes pushes not so gently, as we see in the present chaos in the world and the potential for a lot of life loss. (Or even planet loss).
The principle remains the same. Remain in your Divine Center and the world around you, in any circumstance, will be seen by you as but emanation of the Divine Energy

When you see things that way you create also a whole new world that is by your very being, creating a light-filled place of serenity and peace.
This activity of your spiritual journey can even change the tendency of the world to engage in war and conflict!

How it began – continued

After 10 months on the hippy trail, the Hindu culture like a magnet sucked me in. I became firstly a student of yoga, Hindu philosophy and a guru follower. Then I became a wandering monk, a *sadhu,* and eventually a "mini-guru" myself. During my ten continuous years stay in India, I met a variety of gurus, yogis, holy men and holy women. I travelled the length of the country. Increasingly I was feted, garlanded and was dined in splendor by the prostrating devotees, who admired holy men.

At the end of it all I returned England almost on the spur-of-the-moment. Overnight I felt that to speak, think and dream in

Hindi was ridiculous. Similarly, my wrap-around cloths became trousers and shirts, and I became a normal Englishman again. (I did embark on series of more conventional travels and experiences over time).

I missed out on 10 years of what happened in the Western world during those years in India. On the other hand, especially later in India, I could sit all day long in a perfectly mindless state. Interestingly probably the main reason I left India, is that I became bored with being mindless! Of course, nowadays "mindfulness" is considered wonderful. My attained state had been the ultimate of mindfulness goals!

It took me another 35 years back in the turbulence of life to get back to some of what I had in India. In the so-called normal world, it can be extremely hard to achieve a thoughtless state for most of the day, let alone periods of mindfulness. Unless of course one meditates around the clock. Besides it is unnatural, as we were meant to be active both mentally and physically. What we do need is the ability to switch the mind from *Life and the Universe*, and become a witness to our thoughts.

Why did events happened this way for me?

My answer is that all life is experience and no life experience is separate from the Divine.

Meditation and Truth

If we can initiate nature's own native state and create our own quiet uneventful period, we can control our destiny and future, instead of being like a leaf that is blown, subject totally to events and people around us.

Not that all people feel used or abused by life's "evolutionary direction". We are usually happy to procreate! Interestingly a seeming inability to create a quiet space can be taken as a positive in the world. We are seen as engaged, and therefore quite "sane". Being engaged is often, however, taking what is actually forced upon us by circumstance. We may not admit this. Just we don't like to feel powerless.

Having free time is therefore not always an easily acceptable thing, despite what the self-help books say. So it may be very difficult to create a space in one's busy world, where sitting down becomes possible. It can also be seen as indulging in selfish introspection! What a shock then if you clear time and space, stop agitation, distraction, and wants, and you just feel bored or worse, and all your cravings go ballistic! So much for the newfound freedom.

Free time to meditate etc. is a wonderful and necessary thing, but we also have to be able to deal with it and use it advantageously.

We probably have heard eulogies given to the scientific benefits of meditation, relaxation, or quiet prayer. Just try to sit down for 5-10 minutes in absolute stillness with calm and reposed mind. It can be like trying to tame a bucking bronco. The mind is a wild animal. Or part of a relatively civilized mammal called *human.*

To reach a state of perfect happiness, peace or self-knowledge, may require more application than just sitting in medication for half an hour twice daily. To get to a state of perfect yoga, one needs to be perfect yogi. Maybe it's ok for one who can sit in a cave for months at a time, living on a very sparse diet and not watching any TV. Certainly not the Kardashian 's or Coronation Street!

However, it doesn't really actually matter whether one is in New York, the Himalayas, or the outback. The setting is not too important, although there are optimum environments, diets and guided practices.

One should have access to useful materials. This can vary with one's needs as one progresses. Do you need religion? Medication? (Possibly both!). Then potentially even a noisy place is then doable for meditation to take place. Yes suitable food, water, medicinal herbs, good company, and a bit of finance, always play a part in your search and endeavors on the spiritual path.

To become the controller in terms of spiritual awareness, one needs the ability to sit on a rather different plane completely. The philosophy of *Gyana* or Knowledge, says we are already Divine. (Part of *Vedanta* philosophy). We already have Divine experiences every single moment, and every single moment has a Divine purpose.

However, the path of *Bhakti,* or Devotional path, says that we can't just be living in a "delusion of holiness". (As: "I am already Enlightened"). We need the Grace of an external God, a Higher Power, a personal something we surrender to, who then sorts everything out.

The path of *Karma* or Action, says we need to serve others, including God, guru, or church, to attain a higher state. *Raja* Yoga, (Kingly Yoga), says we need to control the senses, manage all aspects of daily routine, be able to sit in yoga posture, and control the mind. Food and drink is also vital, because intake forms not only the body, but also the mind. What you get rid of is also important. The Truth will always be that. It *Shines* in its own Awareness, regardless of religion, spiritual path, culture, or circumstance. You will then need nothing!

Who AM I? What AM I?

England

I decided after my return to England to continue with some connection to my guru, *Swami Muktananda* and the *Siddha Yoga* group. I have written about Siddha Yoga in previous books. (Basically it's about being "Perfected in Spiritual Practice"). I kept up with them for about 15 years very sporadically without any real connection, and no personal contact with my guru.

I did once go in New Zealand to see a talk by the new guru of his establishment, *Guru Mayi*, who became known as the Hollywood guru. She developed some serious real estate in America, including a university campus. (Turned into a Siddha Yoga center). Otherwise my connection with India and my spiritual identity there was mostly over.

I had spent the last three years of my time in India mostly sitting in a hut in the middle of nowhere, thinking about little in particular. At some point, I pondered over my experiences with all the gurus and the monk lifestyle, and came to the conclusion that I had a different type of life experience awaiting me in the West. This was in New Zealand, where I have spent the last forty years. Perhaps the time was not right for me to be a holy man and renunciate of life forever. I returned to my starting point London at the age of 28, and I'm now writing in my 70's.

In 1977 became a student psychiatric nurse and qualified and registered after three years in England. I was still registered in 2022 and working part time in my registered role. In many ways I became the average man in the street, or after my return, the average guy in the pub. I more or less forgot about my role in India, and even felt vaguely embarrassed by it all, and did not disclose to hardly anyone that I had spent ten years in India!

I enjoyed alcohol, TV, movies, fish and chips, parties and discos. I caught up with my missed youthful years! A wide range of normal activities and interests were pursued.

I immigrated to New Zealand, but also in the 80's had a number of years living in Europe, just travelling around in Spain, France and Andorra, after inheriting a small amount of money. Life was cheap there then and for minimal outlay I was able to spend a whole winter season in Andorra and the Pyrenees mountains skiing.

I did think about my yoga practices occasionally from time to time and also remembered my mantras: the sacred words that I had been initiated into in India. Occasionally I would have periods where my inner meditations would be quite pronounced, although essentially, I carried on my routine of whatever I was into the time. Eventually I began again to accept that the spiritual aspect of my life, if not immediately so, was going to be of major importance to me at some point.

In 1985 I wrote my book *English-Man, Beggar-Man, Holy-Man*, about my journey to India and ten years life there. At the same time I embarked on work, career, marriage, getting money and possessions, driving a car, and re-inventing my love of watching live music bands playing in pubs. I dropped my monk identity, but I never lost my eastern philosophy, even when it was mainly subtly buried somewhere.

This writing, brings past into my present spiritual space: the Goddess inspired learning and teaching space.

The Challenge

Now as we continue the spiritual journey, we find ourselves in a place where we may not need all the same signposts, because we have arrived where we want to be, or we have found a way to know where we are going. At this point we may well not need the references of culture, family, and work, to define ourselves. This may seem scary, may feel like withdrawal, or a loss, but it is actually a new opportunity to have more, not less.

Before the Big Bang: "In the beginning there was the Word".

If you stay with the sacred sounds, you're connected with all the molecules in the universe and are enlightened as a realized human within the milieu that is life. Yes there is suffering, pain, and struggle, but that is life.

Realization is the acceptance of life as it is, as a Divine Creation at all times and for all purposes. We at all times are part of the Divine Creation, just as a drop of water is the same water as in the sea. This is not religion: just what could be the norm of life!

13

Humans have added all the accoutrements of religions and spiritual pathways to the Divine Presence, which is the same for all, regardless of what human add to *It*. You can believe that there are multiple gods, different gods, and/or it's possible to have one "better" God than another, and so forth. (As well as being monotheistic).

So, the spiritual practice is being on a pathway that leaves behind the old and gets the understanding that the body is just: "compartments and bits and pieces". Separate seemingly from the Cosmic Reality, yet actually not separate.

Where humans have a major strength, it is in announcing ones essential: "Divineness not divine-mess"! With this strength it becomes possible to divert from, go around, go through, and go over all the human weaknesses, including addictions, mental health problems, relationship distress, and physical sickness. Even financial distress. (Or especially financial distress). This is not a minor undertaking of course.

Turning everything upside down on its head, opens the individual to unlimited potential. The ego still wants to have a sway and say, "no, no". This is my job, this is my partner, this is my car, etc. etc.

We can move above the level of identification and limitation and find the Truth and Reality. We can't abandon reality, but rather need to work through it, with it, and understand it. Such that it is not one's essential self that is in the way, but one's ego based life.

So, it's not possible then to say that anyone is ultimately bad, or hard to say something is anything as other than a part of that One Unity. Self-centered judgment is usually based on ego preferences! In saying I am not part of the Divine, I will then need constant help, support, and opportunities to get what I can or grab in the struggle to survive. And I may or may not get this from this life - ever!

Maybe initially this view of the all-enveloping Divine is just an idea of the moment, whilst starting on some spiritual path or religious pursuit. These "elevated" ideas, this kind of knowledge and experience don't usually arise of their own. Something happened to trigger this motivation. Then there can be incentive to follow the assistance of a suitable teacher or guru, or other contact that is more than "just human being". Maybe strong feelings of discomfort are initially engendered about such spiritual dimensions as expressed here. It is the nature of the ego to seek safety in what is known.

At some point however life stops being "what you do for yourself", and the Cosmic Will makes things happen, whether we want them or not. We see this in the chaos around in present times. If we don't jump out of the burning house, we will go up in flames. (Unless we put out the fire).

If we don't see the winds of change blowing and except them, we will suffer simply by being dragged into change unwillingly.

It is a choice then to take on board the teachings of the ancient sages and seers, find the sacred and our True place in the universe, align with the divine sounds, or engage in spiritual practices innumerable. It's always as per individual choice, even if initially this is only an impulse to get a taste of some spiritual teachings and pathways.

Even religious "persuasions" may have a role to play!

New Zealand 1981

The old grey Ford Anglia was then 16 years old and it was largely held together by rust, with doors that did not lock or even shut properly. I had done one longer trip in it, but mostly was used in Auckland, where I had spent six months as a staff nurse in a psychiatric unit. However, I set out in it on the spur-of-the-moment to go wherever I was going. I ran away. I left a note. I had recently resigned from my job and I was perhaps in a state of great depression, angst, claustrophobic panic, claustrophobic whatever. I don't know.

I can't explain why I did this and why I caused a lot of pain to a lot of people, including my girlfriend who I lived with. I could not face my life anymore, but I was not suicidal, but I had fleeting thoughts that if I stayed where I was, I might drive off a cliff. I had no plans and no backup plan; I just drove south with a suitcase. When I had been in India as a monk, I was completely free then to act like this and go where I wanted, when I wanted. It had only been 5 years since I return to civilization. I did not think of the consequences or the effect on others. I was seeking happiness, relief, peace, whatever that is. My direction in life then was not conducive to discussion with others about what was in my head. No counselling for me! I probably blocked out reality, or whatever I felt. I had not enjoyed my role as a newly qualified psychiatric nurse. I was not ready to settle down into a relationship. I did not know how to do this!

I carried on to the down the North Island to Wellington. En-route I gave a lift to a Swiss hitchhiker. It was really helpful for me to chat about her life hitchhiking around the country, (which was safe in those days), casual working in Australasia, and living out of a backpack.

I immediately had a picture of how I was going to travel now, and how I wanted to be. Free yes, but obviously unable to deal with whatever mental/psychological demons I was harboring. I stayed in a backpacker's hostel in Wellington. A rundown place, full of youngish people from Europe and Australia, and I was able to define for myself where I was heading, for the next few years.

Justifying the past.

It seems to be a normal tendency to look back and say, "oh I did that, why did I do that, what a mistake", or even, "how stupid of me".

In the deepest realized place, it is not necessary to have examination of what happened.
If you throw out the garbage, the rubbish, it's just going out, and it's not necessary to check every little bit in the rubbish bag.

Consciousness is the underlying substratum of "how it was, how it is, how it will be". Something else, anything else, just does not have any great meaning. Even so we may want to live in what is a bit of a museum and interpret things over and over.

Therefore, to move into the state of realization, is to be in a place which is essentially undefinable and cannot be connected to by words and language. (Even though religions and spiritual teachings try to).

One's own Divinity is already in perfection, and as for what happened and will happen, it's still within that Cosmic

Consciousness.

We are what we think, and when we start think Divine, we start to move beyond "mere human". We become what we think.

It does not mean that the world does not exist. Some philosophers and spiritual practitioners call the world illusory. (*Maya*). That may be just another attempt to explain the inexplicable.

When we experience the Truth of existence, the true reality, we comprehend what I call: *Life and the Universe.*

In the universe we can enter into a nameless space in the ether of the cosmos around us. This is also within our hearts when we meditate. The Divine is not just out there, or not just some god sitting in the clouds growing his beard!
Ideas of God again are the product of history, many religions, and many thoughts of philosophers. Some call it the great Buddhist Void, or *Shunya,* and in Post-Vedic times it was "Existence, Knowledge, Bliss". (*Sat, Chit, Ananda*). The great sages, seers, and teachers say that we are in sync with the truth of God in terms of sound, (becoming form), and can go beyond sound also into the soundless etheric space. (The *Akasha*). In any moment and time this present is what is available, what can be known, and this is where the mind can

expand in mindfulness meditation to become united with the source of all, or one with the Cosmic Self.

It does not matter too much about a journey, as every experience can also be seen as part of the Divine Learning Experience, and be recognized as totally purposeful. (With no experience needing or any judgement to be added on). When we accept who we are in Truth we claim our Divinity. We claim our Oneness with the Higher Power, the Divine Goddess. (Or God, if you insist).

When we do this, we can also begin to demonstrate in our practical lives more than just survival. We move past fear, addictions, depression, anxiety, and whatever it is that troubles us as a human. Again, we accept those experiences of pain through mental struggles as part of Divine Learning. *But* we move beyond them!

If we continue to choose to deny our own Divinity, we are denying the Divine in all. We remain a human who wants God to fix us, or some other "version" to do so. (The Incarnation, the Guru, the Buddha, the Jesus). We want to be fixed <u>and</u> stay human, so that we don't have to take on the enormous responsibility incurred when we fully surrender to Truth.

Most religions will not give you permission! (To be *Free*).

To embody yourself in your true identity is heretic, and certainly you are not given permission, by most of society, to be "allowed" to realize your Divinity throughout your whole physical body. Then it becomes required that you remain in fear. Fear because of separation. Where there is many there is no Unity. When we are one with the Cosmic Being we become fearless.

In fearlessness we lose our anxiety, sadness and our obsessions!

Chapter 2
Slight madness!

Europe 1981 on.

Stepping back again to the time after I had completed my journey around the South Island of New Zealand. This is not an autobiography, but I wanted to give a taste of what was happening for me at the time. This is about the spiritual journey with a brief description of the events that form a "background"

I find it hard to say that the next few years of life were anything special or had anything progressive in terms of the spiritual journey. I worked, I had girlfriends, and spent my spare time rather aimlessly and drank quite a lot of beer

In 1981 I became a staff nurse in Nelsons psychiatric hospital and stayed for eight months. I then was a Youth Hostel Warden in the Southern Alps village of Mount Cook, nestled under New Zealand's highest mountain, in the land of glaciers snow, and much rain.

I spent a year as the House Director of a community for the recovery of the mentally ill in the South Island city of Christchurch. I travelled the length of New Zealand again, this time with a campervan. I forgot about my spiritual self, especially about my time as a monk almost completely, as I became enmeshed in the particular life experiences that I was living through. I guess my spiritual spark was still there, but it was veiled by the outer activities.

I left New Zealand in 1984, and I returned after travels in Australia to England, and went to Wales for a summer to live with my girlfriend, who had accompanied me on some of my travels in New Zealand. This period I see as completing another cycle of 10 years, after 10 years in India, with a return to some spiritual endeavors.

My life at the time in Wales consisted of lazy days spent on the beach, with travels around Wales, and many evenings in pubs. Consequently, I was starting to put on weight. Until the age of 36 I had been skinny as a rake in spite of eating anything and everything. The practice of seven years indulgence since my return from India took effect.

Also, without realizing it, I was starting to rely on alcohol to provide the happiness of my days and evenings. I had not meditated or practiced any yoga for years. Still my physical health was remarkably robust, but level of fitness was becoming pathetic. I was reasonably intellectually active and had some culturally inclined interests.

We drove to the south of France and found opportunities for work immediately in Monaco. A very wealthy English lady required assistance with her elderly husband who had Alzheimer's. Free accommodation, food and a salary! We had our own car and went skiing a lot. Otherwise, food and especially alcohol was very cheap at that time. We were able later to travel in southern Spain and have two weeks skiing in Andorra.

We returned to the UK but came back soon as my girlfriend had a teaching job in Andorra, where we then spent the winter. We had full season passes to a ski field, which was "down the road" from our accommodation. This is when I wrote my book English-Man, Beggar-man. Holy-Man, about my time on the road as a hippy from England to India, and about my 10 years in India as a Hindu monk.

This book never got published, although I tried briefly in the UK. Then I felt incredibly restless and I left my girlfriend and England and went back, planning to go to Australia via New Zealand. I embarked on a new future of work, career, marriage, getting money. I still never really dropped my Eastern philosophy, even when it was mainly at a subtle level. I could say therefore that I have a twin personality, rather than a split personality.

Rajo Guna was predominant?

The Gunas

I try not to repeat the extensive use of Sanskrit words, as in my previous book, which was after all focused around my spiritual practices as a monk in India.

There is however an interesting description in Sanskrit about three qualities or *Gunas* of nature.

If you are into healthy activities, healthy diet, and engaging in spiritual practice, our nature has some "purity". This is *Sattva Guna*. (*Sattva* means "pure").

If we are engaged in the world of pleasure seeking or engaging in life for material benefit mainly, we are *Rajasic* and in *Rajo Guna*.

If we are living in darkness, addictions, suffering deep mental health problems, we are *Tamasik*. Stuck in *Tamo Guna*. In the darkness

Therefore, there are three qualities of nature, and three types of food, three types of activities, and so on.

Have a guess which *Guna* you are sitting in!

A lot of us plough our way through this world through our respective careers, marriage, relationships, social experiences, hobbies, interests, and especially desires. So, *Rajo Guna* predominates.

More History....

Throughout the 80's I was not engaged in a spiritual journey or a programme. However, this was to be a space in time, that changed dramatically back to full acceptance of my spiritual being, my essential Divine Nature, that is also the Truth of all existence, and certainly attainable by all human beings. (That is if this view is accepted and surrendered to through your chosen spiritual pathway and practice).

Several years spent in Europe threw up for me the issue of alcohol and weight gain. I had three cycles of putting on 10 Kg. and then losing that after two months of a low alcohol and low carb diet. At that time, I never drank to significant drunkenness, nor remember any hangovers.

In Europe at that time alcohol was extremely cheap and I drank sometimes daily to 1 to 2 bottles of wine at a time. I had no thoughts then about alcohol as a problem, other than causing weight gain and increasing my appetite. This was to be a key issue for me later in my life! Interestingly when I returned to New Zealand in 1987 my first work position was with a community alcohol service. At that point I was keen on returning to a purer or more spiritual life, and so for some years I remained more interested in meditation than going to bars.

I think in 1987 I felt the dormant yogic flame that had been slowly fading, coming back into my awakening awareness. The sleeping mantras began again to revolve in sluggish brain cells. I even took to sitting down to meditate for brief and infrequent periods.

So as 10 years had gone by in India as a monk, now 10 years had passed in the West in the material net. Now I was back at the beginning of a new phase. The next 10 years were practical because I learnt about my own mental instability, marriage, fatherhood, relationships and career. Even though I was strongly negatively affected at times, (and quite dramatically), I feel lucky to have the great fortune to experience life in such depth of highs and lows, the fascinating and the stimulating, and the painful. Yet so much in development lessons.

Seems to me it all just happened. One of my customs has

been a devotion to the Goddess, since India, where I turned to *Kali, Lakshmi, and Saraswati*. All actually forms of the Shakti, that manifests in our bodies as Kundalini and works through the chakras. (This is covered in depth in "Om Divine Grace"). For me what happens and in *Life and the Universe* is Goddess driven, and thus my writings are also Goddess inspired.

I am playing a role in whatever turns up and I'm sure it will continue to work that way in my best interest. So: "its karma man". Destiny is all, or the will of God is paramount.

But which God?

I was essentially happy with any spiritual "thing" which presented before me and I investigated it all. He or She, God, or Higher Power. I am Multi-faith and have freely participated over the last forty years in Christianity, Buddhism, Baha'i etc. etc. Whatever now helps I do that. (Which is now very refined and also espoused in my writings). I have no issues with anyone's faith or spiritual path. None!

I could not say that I was then self-realized but now my philosophy is that a native natural state is to be Divine and from that perspective it is relevant to talk about being realized as our true state within Cosmic Consciousness. In this space it is not necessary to attain anything with regard to the soul and the outer world.

Gunas – continued

At this point meditation is spontaneous and does not necessarily involve sitting in a quiet room. However, it becomes also natural to enjoy contact with spiritually minded people, who also meditate, or have some devotional philosophy. The realized person doesn't feel the need to journey anywhere on this plane or even to follow any rules that spiritual practice usually mandates.
Nevertheless, the qualities of nature still exist.
Going down dark roads and you're sick of it all? It means you're in *Tamasic* mode

When we are in Sattvic mode we are pure, and we like activities with health giving outcomes, both mental and physical.

This means also we eat simple healthy food and avoid *Rajasic* food. (Think coffee here!). Alcohol is *Rajasic,* but alcoholic drinking is *Tamasic,* when it becomes destructive.

From a realized soul's perspective, the *Gunas* act at all times but the soul is the witness of those activities. So, from that perspective technically we can be Enlightened and yet behave in the mode of any of the *Gunas.* E.g., "the drunken master", as described in some Tibetan texts. (It's theoretical)!

Rajasic persons like the pleasures of life: good food and wine, with "life in the fast lane" a popular goal. Then consequently we suffer physical problems from the minor, such as indigestion, to severe, such as heart, money loss, addictions, and depression/anxiety. We are high sometimes and depressed sometimes. We rage and rant, fueled by desire, and aim for own personal gain.

If we are in *Sattvic* mode we cope with life in equipoise.

The *Tamasic* road is dark, and we may be deeply into addiction, but now at a painful level only. Violent, stupid or destructive become descriptor words.
In *Sattvic* mode though, we may not even be seeking self-realization or engaged spiritually as we maybe are just happy and satisfied enough, and we are lucky to have this personality.

Strangely I have felt more of an urge to turn to the spiritual side as a result of some destructive, negative, depressed, or addictive periods! However, life's journey gives us experience of all the *Gunas*.

Auckland…..

After my return I started looking to resume some of my spiritual practice. I had been a follower of Siddha Yoga, but the

Guru had passed away so I was somewhat hesitant to go along to the branch of the foundation in Auckland. Siddha Yoga refers to yoga that is taught by perfect souls to awaken the latent internal *kundalini* energy or *shakti* and thus enable the practitioner to also become a siddha.

The kundalini is envisaged as the serpent power, dormant in the base of the spine until awakened. The teaching is that with the help of the right guru and mantras/meditation the *shakti* can be awakened and rises up the spine through the various centers or *chakras,* to eventually reach the highest point in the head, when the yogic nectar of blissful self-awareness is realized.

I also saw a poster advertising a weeklong meditation course very near to where I was living, and I decided to go as I knew that I always meditate better in a group situation. Somewhat egoistically, I wanted to see how I felt amongst total beginners, and also to find out what this particular group taught. The sessions were being run by the disciples of Shri Chinmoy, an interesting guru who lived in New York. He ran marathons, lifted very heavy weights, painted lots of pictures and at a very advanced stage of life was performing age record weightlifting.

The teachings within the group were very straightforward and uncomplicated. We were asked to try and simply stop all sorts of thoughts for five minutes or so, then we had to concentrate on breathing, draw in good clean air, and then expelled the "badness" within. Next we concentrated with open eyes on one of three objects on the table, including a picture or the guru. Surprisingly I found after so many years of no formal practice I meditated spontaneously and when I tried to block my thoughts, they stopped completely.

I was not willing to state my attainment at the end of each meditation, when asked to describe how we got on. Everyone was saying how frantic their minds had been. I said that my mind had felt much slower, but that it did seem impossible to be thoughtless.

When I did the open eyed meditation, I concentrated on the picture Shri Chinmoy. As I stared at the photo I became aware of a strong upsurge of *kundalini* energy and certain mantra repetitions occurred in my mind. This helped my swing back to a spiritual life and prompted me to get in touch with the Siddha Yoga group.

I enjoyed my four, weekly sessions with the Chinmoy group. I felt that they put their material over simply, but ably and I saw that some of the new students were benefiting quickly. At the end of the sessions everyone was told that they would have to enroll, to continue further.

This entailed filling up the form and having a Polaroid picture taken. The picture would be sent to the guru in New York, where he would meditate on the new student through the photo and guide them in the future meditations. Not all students were to be accepted we were told, but those who were rejected would be guided in other suitable directions.

The idea of not being able to continue with this group without enrollment did not appeal to me. I am critical about religion or spiritual groups when they are not open and free or allow unimpeded participation without pressure.

Although most churches, temples, guru, and groups that I have been involved don't stipulate immediate "enrolment", I know that they all tend to seek some form of commitment eventuality. Also, the meditation and yoga groups derived from India can be seen as part of the Hindu religion, though a lot of the followers would not want to see themselves as Hindus.

For myself I am Multi-faith so this issue is irrelevant, and I have followed whatever I wanted, and was not swayed by sales techniques of the proponents of whatever group or cult was being promoted. Make no mistake though, yoga with *mantras gurus, kundalini, and chakras,* are all basically part of the Hindu religion, even when they have been watered down and sanitized to meet a secular Western market. Philosophies, religious and spiritual practices should not be grabbed to become the property of any group or sect, and channeled into moneymaking enterprises. Due recognition of their source is good.

Keystone phrases.

Firstly, let's take the word *enlightenment*
Delete!
Then the word *realization or self-realization*
Delete!
Why?
A lot of zeros have no value, but if the number one is place before the zeros, then we have 1 million, (for six zeros).
I have a body I have a mind.

I have relationships, careers, and so forth plus my spiritual bit as the soul.

My spiritual beliefs may be giving me a sense of being enlightened but remember this word is not in favor.
I have recovered or am in recovery from mental health, addictions, physical issues, relationship issues, career issues.
I can use the word "in recovery" because this is the case as long as I have a body and mind.
I am where I am now due to strong efforts: searching and learning.

The spiritual practices led me to a space, a Higher Room, from where I was able to connect with my strengths and resilience, with which I could achieve my recovered/recovery status. (Really about recovery from enmeshment in *Maya*).

We need a new word then which encompasses "perfection", that is spiritual, (and religious if you really need it), but also acknowledges worldly, physical and mental "perfection."

Perfection here is a sense of confidence, capability, and ability to resolve life issues as far as realistically possible, and to feel fully spiritually developed (or fully immersed in the spiritual journey).

It's a place where all the issues of *Life and the Universe*, have been re-identified into the Divine Truth for the human in individual form. With the personality intact! Fears are resolved and individuals can sit in their own Divine Space, Higher Power/room

Technically then what happens is simply the ongoing experiences of life which happen automatically over the course of time, as karma outcomes.

That realistically enlightened individual no longer acts to get, make, achieve, but rather will experience, (the results of past actions). Teaching or service to others may still take place as per one Deity inspired influence

My new phrase then is: *Practical Enlightenment.*
Also, I like *Realistic Realization*

Now this is a sense of being - simply experiencing life, (as if the train ran out of fuel but keeps on roiling).

This is what is happening to one, around one, automatically as a result of past actions
It doesn't mean the person doesn't shower or eat etc. because these are also activities set up previously to perpetuate the life lived, and thus "roll" automatically.
It does not mean one doesn't go to work or doesn't remain in marriage or other relationships.

Again, these are set up and continue at their own pace under their own steam unless of course they spontaneously, naturally drop away.

There is no striving either to change things the way they are
they are
It is as it is
But there is no issue, no complaint, no fear, no anxiety, or regret.
This is *Practical Enlightenment and Realistic Enlightenment.*

Therefore, I write a reflection of what happened to me in my journey through life which was in its foundation a spiritual journey combined with, entwined with, the realities of life, relationships, work, money, and whatever comes under the heading:

Life and the Universe.

Then throughout life experience comes spiritual reflection and awareness, entwined and connected.
Generated through the influence: Goddess inspired....

Auckland ....

After group sessions with Chinmoy meditation, I got in

touch with the Siddha Yoga center in Auckland and began to attend their chanting meditation sessions. They had a permanent hall installed with photos of Swami Mucktananda, (deceased) and the guru who succeeded him, Gurumayi, the "Hollywood guru". These photos formed the temple images for worship, and indeed use of photos/pictures for worship is common in Hinduism.

The photos are taken as representing the guru who thus still "leads" the congregation and is envisioned as sitting at the front of the devotees, who seek to imbibe the atmosphere of the guru's Shakti whilst chanting or meditating.

I found the atmosphere similar to the atmosphere I felt way back in 1972 when I stayed ten months in the ashram in India. There was a strong feeling of something in the air, hard to explain, but it was easy to meditate and chant, (the Hindu equivalent of hymns), in the peaceful atmosphere of the center. For Westerners, Hindu derived worship is not always so palatable even amongst the followers, though it's part of the package that comes with the Eastern guru.

I did find the chanting and other ceremonial activities to be uplifting, though I guess that the permanent followers of the center probably got more out of it than I did. I did find also my thoughts were positive about the new guru, and also, I liked the meditation methods, including watching the thoughts and remaining in the true state as their witness. This is: "I am not the mind and body but the witness of all my activities and thoughts".

The main pathway of this center though is Siddha Yoga, and

the *Shaktipaat* of the guru. By devotion to and focus on the guru, one receives the *shakti* that enters the devotee downwards into the *chakras* and awakens the *kundalini*. In India this was very obvious & promoted heavily at the ashram. Devotees would go into trances, dance, and engage in bodily writhing and other manifestations, consequences of receiving the *shakti*. When I first went to the ashram, outside of Mumbai, I thought it was "all a load of rubbish"!

After several weeks in the ashram and some brief *darshans*, (being in the gurus presence), I found myself dancing ecstatically and involuntarily. That is why Swami Muktanand became so famous in the West, and he set up centers around the world. People would come to him, and without even accepting him as their guru, would begin to have the bodily manifestations of "kundalini arising". I have never seen anything like it since, and certainly not on a mass level. Fascinating!

For a while the Siddha Yoga Foundation was a major player in the world of East meets West spiritual organizations. Unfortunately, Swami Muktananda, when in his 70's, attracted a lot of negative press, due to the discovery of his sexual activities with young devotee girls! Not sure what happened there, but I had by then moved on from that organization as a source of inspiration for my spiritual journey.

The people I were living with at the time were part of a somewhat different group, although connected. The guru of the group was called then Da Love Ananda. He had been a follower initiated by Swami Muktananda, and went off separately to form his own organization in America. He also became very famous for some quite negative reasons but also produced a large volume of works which I found very interesting.

I maintained my connection with that group for quite a few years to come, as I was also had friendship connections with some members of the group. I never joined up but I did enjoy going to the events from time to time and I actually got a lot out of dipping in an out of selected works and reading what their guru said. I did not accept his writings where he just wrote profusely that he was the only means for anyone's salvation. (He called his method, "only by me, through me"). It was a bit like Christ saying one could only come to the father through him. My multi-faith view sees this as limiting the *Truth*.

Over the next ten years and more I visited various groups for a while, explored Bahaism, and started to resume some of my connection to the Anglican Church. A close family friend encouraged me to attend some rather more evangelical Christian events, often in very large very well attended venues, where they had bands and hymns were on screens.

Not really my "cup of tea".

Over 30 years I developed a habit of occasionally attending a Sunday service at the Auckland Anglican Cathedral, or other venues if overseas, where I receive Holy Communion. I enjoy the ceremonials, the liturgy, and the choir. I see Jesus Christ as a holy guru worthy of my deepest respect. This is not my main spiritual path way, and I have no concerns about what others think, as I am

Multi-Faith, and I do what I want in terms of my own spiritual journey. That is my business and I have no time whatsoever for any form of fundamentalism, or even religious people trying to tell me that their religion, or belief, is the only way. Equally I totally accept what others follow or believe in.

The years from 1990 to 2000 were taken up by my roles on a whole as a husband, a father and with my psychiatric nursing career. (Possibly material for another book)!

This era took me out to the age of fifty plus.

During this period, I struggled at times with depression, anxiety, and alcohol, although essentially, I was quite functional. My spiritual practices remained very important to me, but at times became over-shadowed by my struggle to maintain a grip on stability at all levels.

I realize now how I became spiritual in the first place. Because I struggle with life and it seems that the more I struggle and fail, the more spiritual I become or rather the more desperate! I also had a problem with living life on life's terms & have always had an inner urge to "run", (away). This desperation, looking back, had been with me since the age of 11 when I believe I became clinically depressed.

I have noted that my time in India may have been extended due to a clinical chronic depression, of which I was not aware, but which kept me in place as a monk for so many years. My real journey then has not been only about being spiritual, but rather about overcoming, the experience of being a human being, who was struggling in many ways. In time I had some success at all levels, including mental and psychic, so that I could be spiritually realized and humanly realized.

This is where I am now: being in *Practical Enlightenment (or Realistic Realization)*. This state or stance has taken me more than 40 years since leaving India to obtain. It has taken me years of struggling with depression, alcohol or addictive type behaviors, and trying multiple therapeutic modalities, as well as medications.

It is taken me forty years to understand that I carry with me an underlying dysthymic depression, (a chronic low mood disposition or even personality).

I learnt that I could manage my mood most of the time very successfully with certain natural medication. Also I have understood that I have susceptibility to severe attacks of depression, but it's only in the last five years that I have realized that the severity is now seasonal. This seasonal affective disorder, (S.A.D.), I have successfully managed so manage well and thrive as a human being whether or not I have a spiritual or religious practice

I have also realized that I always drank alcohol when depressed beyond a certain point, as I then no longer cared to live any more. By drinking over some years as a medication solution, I became quite naturally dependent. Also, when severely depressed, I understand that I can become dependent on anything that can take away the pain and suffering.

Now I have recourse to a very small amount of a specific

medication that gives benefits in S.A.D. (only if needed), plus light therapy, and that allows me to overcome low mood during the winter. Plus, the addition of herbal adaptogens at other times enables me to remain in a stable physical and mental space at all times. (I had to research what the top expert's in America recommend for S.A.D., and push to get this for myself in New Zealand).

However, it has taken me many years to find exactly what works for me and what works for me may not work for someone else. At the time of writing, I work in the mental health field as a registered nurse, and as a professional I know that I can't just pass on what works for me to some of the people I work with. However, I can pass on, in my writings, the spiritual activities which have given me the spiritual enlightenment part of my being.

Chapter 3
Practical Enlightenment

Surrender

There seems to be some idea that spiritual surrender is about giving up our attachments

This seems more like acceptance, where we accept life "as it is" Then, we sit in our Divine knowledge and whatever happens is *Prarabdha.* (A Sanskrit word for the accumulated force of past karma). This where a *Brahma Gyani* sits. (Knows themselves, as one with the Cosmic Soul, the *Brahman*). Hence the word *Gyana,* which is knowledge of the *Brahman,* the Cosmic Soul. (The individual soul is called the *Atman*).

When you surrender spiritually, you stop making or seeking solutions to the uncontrollable. In the 12-step model its: "my life became uncontrollable". (Hence then the need to surrender to a Higher Power). To stop seeking solutions also seems to be about acceptance. Surrender is willful acceptance and yielding to a dominating force and its will. Acceptance helps you accept the good and bad equally.

However, surrender also is to become aware of the Divine as oneself, with the Higher Power's energy *within*, and to accept it. It involves a shift in belief or approach to the spiritual journey, and is about "Who am I?"
Is this a catalyst for enlightenment?

Trust, and faith that there is a Divine Force seems to be a pre-requisite for surrender. "I believe that God will help me through this". This requires some awareness of options generated by the usual questioning that goes until a belief in the Divine co-exists with faith in your spiritual teachers.

> *Not just: What is this all about?*
> *But also: What do I do (as service)?*

The act of surrender requires some practical substance also. Mediation, prayer, chanting, using a mantra etc. What is the single most powerful tool you use on your spiritual journey? You can't think "I don't have to do anything else", and not do the practice required.

By turning your awareness away from normal activity and settling the mind, you can reconnect with your inner space. In the silent spaces beyond thoughts, you surrender to a Sound, the Cosmic Sound. Just as there is noise in life, there is noise in realization. It is very different though and can't be explained, only experienced.

You submerge your ego, which remains, but is transformed into identity as the Divine, where there is the bliss of Oneness. (When you can hear then the Cosmic Sound).

If all else fails, just pray for surrender. It doesn't matter who or what you pray to, it matters only that you are willing. The intention to surrender will allow its own release, and who knows, maybe there is an old man up there sitting in the clouds! (For me it's the Goddess, but I'm not saying my beliefs are any less "naïve")! Anything that helps with letting go of fear and unending desire is worth a try.

Again, the small self, the individual "me," is not capable of dropping its own sense of ego, even though the *Atman* is intertwined with the *Brahman*. (Just as water is water, whether in a drop or in a sea). Maybe the "rock bottom" of the addict or a state of impasse, or "the darkest night", triggers some transcendence. It is a pity that it may have to occur this way! A realization "I simply cannot do it, can't win, can't complete, can't change the situation".

Something has to change, even if is occurring within a state of mental disorder. Someone will come to attend to you even if temporarily, involuntary, as when mental health becomes life threatening.

If however, you trust the Divine then the Divine Grace leads from darkness to light.

When we agree to participate in the process of surrender to our Higher Power or place our lives in the hands of God then we are met by the Divine Force. The change occurs when there is willingness to access and seek the Truth. This makes us available to be witnessed and to witness. We can then stop hiding and leave the past shames and fears behind. The Divine Self as the individual soul can then be healed by Divine Grace.

Maybe medication, therapy, rehabilitation, or other treatments will work.
Maybe

Or rather all the healing opportunities in the world may be helpful "to a point'. Maybe

The issue finally is about being at another level. This is not just about praying to seek the god, the higher power, or one's deity. It's about being in one's own Higher Power, being in the Divine Self and experiencing Divinity in human bodily form.

We have been claimed by a situation where we may live very fearful human lives, whilst at the same time seeking redemption, solutions to suffering within and without our personal lives.

There is a necessity, or a choice, or we are pushed to move "past the past". To release all of life in a higher way through the encounter with one's own Divine Self. The rubbish or garbage is put out, and there is no need to check and go through it all. Just throw it out! Let it go to leave the darkness behind. Freedom from self-condemnation, anger or righteous action, becomes grounded and light, and only then is the darkness absent.

Some would say that the material reality is an illusion. The Sanskrit word for this is *Maya,* the delusional dreamlike transitory life experience. The true *Maya* though is that we believe there is happiness all around us. In success, money, and even relationships.

The Buddha indicated that "all life is suffering". Thus, life and free will at a high level seeks not to totally alleviate personal strife, but to see the Truth of life's journey as having an ultimate benefit for all. Cancer is not eliminated. Mental health disorders are not eliminated. Poverty is not eliminated. War is not eliminated. We just don't participate from the same angle any more, we have a radically different perspective and understanding of what the universal Divine Consciousness is. Which cannot be in truth separate from anything or anyone.

Either this "consciousness" is homogeneous, or it doesn't exist for a benefit, (as it would not then be anything of spiritual value)! The ending of delusion, the end of the chase of dragons and dreams, can be celebrated. Accomplished by agreeing and participating in the spiritual journey, and that can be accomplished by being on a path of one's personal choice.

There are signposts, teachers, and guides to help us.

Even that the parts of religion that have not been corrupted can serve a purpose on this journey. It's all available if we seek it, but more than that it will only work if we let it.

That is where the challenge of surrender lives!

Acceptance

The deal with surrender is that there follows acceptance.

Our God, Higher Power or Divine has a plan with exactly what we need to be given when we need.

This seems scary!

What if it's not true!

What if I don't like what I get?

It's a bit like going to a restaurant having to eat what is placed in front of oneself, instead of ordering.

What if I get non-vegan?

Or fish?

The good thing is that confusing choices can be released. What do I do about my marriage? What do I do about my job?

The Divine ensures that each step is revealed to one who makes the surrender and waits.

Answers come with surety as the inner voice, which only makes good sense if it's a true voice.

Thus a word of warning. Those who are mental health professionals are well aware of the delusional content of the mind in states of sickness, when thoughts can be misleading, dangerous and life-threatening.
It may pay to check things out with a suitable professional person, guide, or therapist, if indicated.

It's also a good idea to do so with a health professional if one is susceptible to unraveling or is vulnerable to a mental health condition.

The issue is not really about what will happen to you, or what you will do, or how your five-year plan will work out. It's about sitting in a space where fear and anxiety about, *Life and the Universe* is alleviated.
Of course we desire, we want great things, and that lottery win.
Being in the Divine place is not about forceful relinquishing of our desires or even addictions.
It's about being in a space where it is natural to accept the fullness of life "as it is", and thus the needs and wants disperse, vanish or become irrelevant.

Gratefulness for what we have not regret for what we haven't got.

Acceptance is that there is enough, and I can share fully what I have got.

I don't have to win to the detriment of others. (Maybe sport is different).

Being one with the Divine Self will enable outcomes of benefit without or beyond limitation.

Far greater things can happen.

There still will be in counters in life that confuse, and cause fear and anxiety but again the Divine Design is that we learn.

Everything is included as part of the spiritual journey.

Thus desire can be re-purposed and re-understood.

Something to not fight against. Something purposely placed in the correct position in the scheme of things.

Enlightenment gained

I regained a sense of control over circumstance, which is influenced and self-regulated by my understanding of the workings *of karma and prarabda,* about which I write. This means a complex awareness of both the inevitability of some events and the endless possibility of change. Ultimately total self-responsibility leads away from the known spiritual pathways and into the depths of Divine Grace!

I had a feeling of being powerless over my human condition seemed to prevail for quite a few years. Although this was for a seemingly lengthy period I believe it gave me eventually a better understanding with better ability to be realized at all levels of the mind/body, *whilst fully in the world.*

Practical Enlightenment or Realistic Realization.

My own practice led me to a state where I had the opportunity and ability to control not only major elements of my own life but also that of others if I wished, through yogic powers or *siddhis.* Somewhat strangely when I had taken those "powers" from India into the everyday life of marriage, children, & career, I found that my spiritual energy seemed to have faded.

Here I developed an understanding of my philosophy. Where realization of *"Aham Brahma Asmi"*, (I am the Cosmic Soul), is a completely different and more powerful awareness. This could be called enlightenment or realization. However, I consider that true enlightenment occurs only on completion of the spiritual journey and all components of the worldly experience journey.

Looking back some questions arise regarding my degree of spiritual attainment. I spent 10 years in India as a monk, and thirty plus years of struggling with mental health and addiction issues. Had I then attained a state of self-knowledge and achieved M*oksha*? (Moksha is equivalent to *Nirvana* which is more common term in Buddhism. Moksha means freedom from the cycle of rebirth, or it just means freedom from this trouble human existence). Release into what? Furthermore, had I found my own true religion and philosophy that can even be substantiated, (somewhat), scientifically, and which can be now said to be lasting and permanent benefit all-round?

On leaving India I had developed a clearly defined Hindu derived Vedanta philosophical look on life which did not change with in the passage of time. This was not about having multiple gods, sitting in temples, but was about a very monotheistic outlook that was or even ultra-monotheistic possibly. I find the Vedanta philosophy enables a deeps sense of satisfaction. That I have something that is *Truth Unlimited*, which is unaffected or swayed by any or all religious type beliefs. It is about oneself as the Divine and about Maya, the illusory and transient suffering filled nature of *Life and the Universe*. Vedanta though seemingly nihilistic or fatalistic, has given me the means to develop calmness and equipoise, and helped alleviate the ups and downs of life.

Is Grace Divine?

Human beings with intelligence may reflect that something is missing, without understanding the spiritual aspect necessarily, let alone the meaning of *Life and the Universe*. However, even at a therapy level they can be an understanding that you don't have to do anything really arduous, you don't have to "retrain", and you don't have to like people, or be liked. Think about getting the life that's going to be source of your Eternal Bliss. (Or some sanity in the case of therapy).

What is the issue with marriage, children, and career? (In regard to both spiritual practice & personal sanity)? Is desire for a new car, kitchen, or overseas travel a bondage or just normal? It comes down to whether this Is freedom for you Do you want the bondage-based years, and years of life only leading to a death where you can take your "toys" or wealth? If so carry on!

If not, there may not be another way. (Other than Divine Grace). If you have a better way I must have already read your books!

Alternatively, if you are already Divine, you are already free. It is your own true nature. If you have removed the veil of ignorance, generated through worldly obsessions. We are all bound to the law of action, bound to death, (and taxes), but karma is not our master. Choose the Divine self & you become the Master or keep trying your own pathway. Even if you falter & struggle or kind of give up, that's when your ego takes a hit.

What about the atheist? There will be an alternative way if you look. The Vedanta philosophy can be interpreted in a non-God manner, as indeed can much of Buddhism.

Without discipline nothing much will happen. The addictions, obsessive behaviors and negative attitudes, are not bad. They are just about being stuck and the spiritual practice goes nowhere. Then a different program, which is monitored and supported, is needed, with perhaps professional or "sponsor' support. A position where a decision to have a counsellor, guru, or sponsor is a statement of decision to change.

The ego can say: "no I can't do it I'm just a hopeless drunk", "my depression is too deep", or "I am unable to escape an unhappy marriage". Maybe it's really about being just plain too scared, (to change)? Then one has to agree to cede the power of the ego & maybe even to accept the loss of the ego. Then surrender to receive the Divine Grace. Fix your mind on God your Higher Power or Deity to do this.

The Grace is there, you have just got to get hold of it, or rather not get hold of it, but position yourself where it flows and be in the stream. This logically is an activity that makes things happen, by allowing Grace to flow. Do some prayers, try a mantra, and learn to meditate.

Another way around any doubts & confusion around the spiritual pathway needed is to understand that we are covered in ignorance due to the presence of Maya, the "illusory" nature of the world. Lost in a recurrence of our dream, we are just in our ignorance, and we just can't see the Truth. Life goes around & around & we are always back to where we started. This ignorance of Truth is our normal self, just our usual everyday personality-based ego. When we choose to surrender the ego, we get the Grace.

Easy on paper!

Another problem lies with promoting human attributes to a computer type vagueness, as in: "I'm just cruising along", that mostly equates karma with only outcomes, but no real meaning about it all. It's perhaps a bit of a leap to think about the Divine Grace as belonging in the field of an impersonal, or atheistic type belief, but of course it is worse to just be a robot following the herd, as per the rules of evolution. (We are then created only by the developing or evolving human mind - no intelligence required).

It may also seem if we develop more insight that we can attain more by determination to continue the struggles, (to succeed)." Eventual though in my belief we will end up having to say: "my struggles got me nowhere" but hopefully then this leads to: "the Divine Grace illuminated me". A bit confusing perhaps if we have to wait until it flows "down". (Grace that is). What's the point of doing anything? Can some get it, but another does not? (No & no!).

Grace is pretty certain if you seek it, but why is it placed sometimes as the ultimate, as "out there somewhere". Why is it fairly often proposed in religion as being the only way to achieve salvation? The Buddha did not seem to speak much of Divine Grace, whereas in the worlds of other religions, scriptural announcements about being chosen through Grace seem fairly prominent.

This view is not the foundation of the Vedanta philosophy, where it is proclaimed that our natural state is what drives the urge to attain salvation. (Because our no-salvation did not, cannot, & does not really exist, apart from in our "dreaming void" of Maya. In this philosophy the sinner and the saint, good and bad, rich and poor, are equal in terms of being part of the Cosmic Consciousness, (the *Brahman*), expressed as the individual soul, (the *Atman*).

All religions are clear that we can be saved in some form and get into a kingdom of some form of God enveloped environment or presence, but only if we are "good". If the essence of Truth is within our souls associated with the heart area, it seems like that is all about being totally self-responsible, and about trying one's best to do good deeds, but not dependent solely on them. By all means serve others and pray to one's Deity. So, religion may have as closely intertwined doctrine of Grace, inseparable from the search and the seeker, who is seeking truth within. Thus, that grace seems to render self-responsibility nil and void at times.

The agreement is generally that as humans we are in some sort of a mess, & that we need to get out of this, usually crafted as environmental or political or cultural terms. Spiritual view may still be about whether this is seen as be freedom from sin and placement in heaven or breaking the bonds of ignorance and preventing future reincarnations. Or some other perspective. (Religions can have some view that the Divine is actually within, as well as without. Usually, the heart is designated the place for it all to happen).

So, there is possibly no need for Divine Grace!
If we could all achieve Nirvana, salvation, enlightenment, through our own normal natural efforts then we might only need the help of a few teachers or gurus or just help from Google!

Chapter 4
Post – enlightenment?

Goddess Power

The Goddess represents both Maya in the whole world of human suffering, searching and pleasure seeking, and also represents the link back to the Universal Being, which is formless, pervasive Cosmic Consciousness. (Some people call it God). The Goddess is the energy or Shakti represented by the Kundalini force, which rises up the spine with the human awakening, to break through at the crown of the head, so as to allow the liberation of the soul.

The Goddess is also the focus of the Tantric way that includes the world in worship. Instead of exclusion, there is inclusion of "money, food and sex". (Which is in need often of being dealt with appropriately). The Goddess is the link or a means of transferring human identity to Divine identity by generating the understanding of what my gurus and guides are talking about.

Now my awareness is that there is no religion, or even spiritual belief that I have to defend. I also do not have to follow any path, but I am simply aware of my own choices in this matter. I have opened up to any religious or spiritual experience that helps and accept the need for the many forms that religion and spirituality take. This then has led me to where I am now, in talking about Shakti & *Devi*, (Goddess as opposed to *Deva* - God).

If this does not make sense, then what does make sense?

There must be something, some way of living that makes sense in our world, such as that our spiritual being is our essence, & leads us to something super-special. Religion may have some answers, and historically has done the job quite well for a lot of people

However perhaps modern life views of religion are result of finding out the truth of religious organizations & decrees. This has added up to finding out that you have a Picasso, but it's fake! People may have also enjoyed their faith but discovered it's like black and white TV, (which we had in the 50's). Then we discover there is color TV!

Religion now does not seem to provide the answers to a lot of people in the Western world. In the Eastern worlds, religion is still a foundation of a culturally based society. That also is changing quite rapidly now we have instant worldwide Google, Facebook, and YouTube. As we know just being in the world, even if our culture is still solid, does not automatically resolve some fundamental doubts & questions.

I bypass all spiritual practice hype & confusion, by a surrendering process. That is to leave it up to the Goddess, or rather give it over to the Goddess. This can be replicated of course in whatever one's pathway or religion is, and as I am multi-faith I have absolutely no issue whatsoever with doing the same process through any religion or any spiritual practice. I don't have any issue or energy to discuss the benefits of one way or another, and I am simply not interested in debating my religion/s, (or politics). It is irrelevant, get on with the job, and attain Enlightenment and Realization.

I discovered that we all walk towards our Nirvana, and simply our world of experience is set up to provide the necessary learnings. (Who made this so)? We can sit back when we see life "as it is and ourselves as we are". This does not cure or even deny room for change or personal growth. Just that one is able to work, without being affected dramatically by success or failure. Also, that any objective is already present as the perfect Self. (The *Atman as one with Brahman*). The journey, the effort is also the goal. Do you live in terms of being self-realized, when what we want is already achieved, and anything else is also certainly achievable? Then one's way of living automatically changes to one of living in the light, and one gets out of the darkness.

Two key things for me have made me interested also in the channeled teachings of the Guides. (See books by Paul Selig where he channels the teachings). Firstly, the goal as expressed is to be free of fear, totally and unconditionally, as when one is in the light in the darkness doesn't exist. As I have struggled with life's fears & anxieties, this has been my goal. If I am honest, when I was a monk in India for those ten years, I was probably still enmeshed in more core human fear of "life & death". Secondly, I see the teachings as being completely open to anyone at any stage, without any necessary background. No previous knowledge. My time as a monk counts for nothing, my spiritual practice today to counts for nothing! Unless I make the free choice of surrender to the purpose of living in the Higher Rooms, and unconditional accept my birthright to be a Divine being. (Under all circumstances). This ties neatly in with my surrender to Goddess Shakti as the world made manifest, & to me acceptance of personal Divinity, via the Vedanta teachings.

So, in some respects this combines both a personal deity with an impersonal deity, and some "scientific" practice of working with bodily centers using the yogas of meditation, mantra and yoga postures. As well as a focus on chakra energies to connect my mental & physical body to the Goddess Shakti. This may seem contradictory but has been in practice from ancient times as per the writing of the sages and seers in India. They espoused lofty philosophies but also worshiped their chosen or *Ishta* Deity. (Devi, Rama, Shiva etc).

For some time the Guides were my gurus for the Gnostic part of my practice. Previously I had human gurus that guided my practice as a monk and into later years. Also, I have been guided or helped by a number of therapists, in regards to psychological mental components of my life. It's all about what works!

So, still a core component of my spiritual practice has been the worship of the Goddess as my personal

Deity, which in practice has entailed engaging in *Kundalini Yoga.* This for me is working with the centers of the body, the c*hakras,* through which the *kundalini* passes as it arises from the base of the spine. This practice is also about Shakti, the Divine Goddess energy, which can be invoked using mantas, especially "seed" mantras. A devotion to the Goddess alongside my monotheistic or non-dualist philosophic practice. The mantras though are the key activity, and these refer to specific goddess forms, (of the one Divine Shakti). As they are directed to specific chakras in the body, this repetition of mantras purifies and brings light to the human realm. They also work subtly on mental health issues, addictions and obsessions.

The work of the Divine Goddess is about spinning us into the web of Maya, seemingly on the surface. Then to trip us into mundane activities, but really to eventually liberate, as the Divine works happen in the world, and not in some cave or monastery.

We are led to:
Practical Enlightenment or Realistic Realization.
Eventually.

As long as we are "on the pathway". We are all full of

subconscious material relating to needs and desires but need to experience life through the physical persona in order to transcend the ego. Of course, free will and choice is involved, and I had to make a choice to surrender to this version Higher Power, even if it was born of desperation. The mantras that I repeat as part of my spiritual way led my individual self into an awareness of Universal Self, expressed as the Cosmic Sound. Eventually this sound can be experienced beyond meditation and bought right down through the chakras of the body to the toes and into all aspects of my life, "out there". *Life and the Universe.*

Becoming free

My years long ago in isolated huts and villages, gave me time and space to consolidate a core foundation Awareness. However, I came to realize one part only of my spiritual journey, which was of a reclusive isolative nature. That I was 50% complete or 50% incomplete! It did take me another forty years to resolve the rest.

The underlying and sometimes automatic subconscious thread of devotion to God still worked for me to enable a Grace that made practical the therapy, recovery, mental wellness, and strength or fortitude. The

Western world and my ordinary existence of family, work, and finances have enabled me to understand how the esoteric Eastern based philosophy of Shakti is providing true understanding or spirituality. It's at all levels, through all cultures, and also props up the formless non-dual concepts of Vedanta enabling it to be, not just for monks, as traditionally it had been.

We should be now in the moment, being present, and if we are not really feeling it we should be using all the spiritual practice tools at our disposal. Prayer, mantra, meditation, or other means. Then there is no excuse, only self-responsibility. There is only the requirement to do what is needed moment to moment and "get on with it". Deal with it, function and provide solutions, as far as one can. Beyond that we are at the mercy of our God!

The Guides say we are all Divine, and we all live in a Divine world that is undifferentiated in the sense that this perspective/belief is for everybody. All persons have equal opportunity as they are all by birthright Divine beings, in their bodies and human lives. This is way more accessible than Vedanta which was really the domain of sannyasins and swamis, initially in India. It is still often seen as being a philosophy in the domain of renunciation and monastic leanings.

Vedanta says *Aham Brahma Asmi.* I am the Divine or Cosmic Consciousness and the world is *Maya.* (Illusory). This can be seen as religion without a God, and has similarities to Buddhism, which evolved in India post *Upanishads.* (The scriptures defining Vedanta, which were written at a later stage of the *Vedas.* (*Veda* plus *anta* = Vedanta). The Guides speak through their writing & the words that come across sounds to me very much like my philosophy of the Vedanta, placed into much more modern terminology and perspective. The goal the Guides propose is to stay or live in the Higher Rooms where one lives as one's higher self, which then allows all the answers to life questions to flow spontaneously.

The Guides words have made it very clear to me that this "I am Divine', is for the present times for all. This is what we need now in what is a chaotic world of darkness. I had never seen my divine Shakti in a concrete vision but have felt the presence for a long time of a male spirit that has guided me or at least supported me. This personal presence completely resonated in agreement with what the Guides were saying, and I could re identify with elements of my "monk person" that I had held for so many years. Then I started to feel the female guide spirit & now there is a combination. (Read on for more about this later).

Also seek the guru within as well as without. The Vedanta teachers say that when we ask ourselves, who am I, we are trying to find out what the true nature of the "I" is. Not mind, not body, but an unchanging entity, that remains constant through childhood to old age. It is the self within the Atman which is the same substance as the Cosmic Soul. All the teachers of this way point out not only the importance of the guru, but also of the Deity that one surrenders to. The guru within will also be a guide who directs towards the highest energies.

One of my gurus in India, Swami Muktananda, was somewhat scathing when I turned up to his ashram in my robes speaking Hindi and looking like a swami. He said in about two sentences: "you're always going to be English, no matter how Indian or Hindu you try to be. And what's wrong with Christianity"? I did not really except he had said those words. I pretended he hadn't. It took me a long time to see what he said was absolutely true.

With attraction to the Divine comes a natural tendency to serve others, & that is for me a keystone of Christianity. It is in place, even if I have been a bit driven at times by excessive, obsessive, or pleasure-seeking type common human behaviors. I can see the goodness in the mistakes I made, but now I can say it's no longer about mistakes, they are just enriching experiences. I prefer to call them learning experiences. As long as I can still serve others then I am still on the right path!

Though quite different from Christion views, the marble form of the idol in the temple is a means to help with spiritual practice. It is not worship of a piece of marble, rather a useful means of purifying a psycho emotional mental deficit, and an activity done with a view to developing concentration and awareness. The purpose of any external devotion is that the true nature of ones Divine self becomes self-evident into all levels of one's human form and existence.

Although I feel and talk of the Divine Spirit including religious reference, it is also useful to place it in view of life experiences in terms of mental wellness, addictive behaviors, and pleasure seeking lifestyles. (All the baggage that goes with normal human behaviors out there in life and the universe). The real need is to remain focused on the goal of coming to the Divine awareness, and then find the inner true guru, & to what you know you are in essence.

Your guides: they are you and have purpose as separate, only to take you to awareness of the Truth, which coincides with the loss of the lower self through transcendence of your ego tendencies. Then you don't need gurus, you are the Guru!

This is the wakening to the day of the light. Whatever religion or spiritual pathway has got you so far. The purifying benefits in terms of ego transcendence leads to dimming or disappearance of the psycho emotional and addictive tendencies that cause so much havoc in so-called civilized society.

Because I see the Universal Spirit as manifesting through the power of the Shakti or Goddess creative Maya, I accept that the energy of Shakti has to be brought into real life. I see the need to deal with and understand this energy as essentially a female aspect of Divinity, without negating the other male aspects of energy in the cosmos. I.e. Is the Cosmic Consciousness – male?

Transactions of ego in all matters, (including psychosexual, and romantic), after I left India, required of me to accept the mental distresses experienced. That meant that the type of existence I continued with for many years thereafter submerged my spiritual journey into a more common mode of survival. I forgot any kudos I had gleaned as an ex-holy-man. I think I had to become a humble-man not a holy-man.

Life events can be seen as an action directed by a

force, based on which choice is made by the individual. Such choices, and then endeavors, range from choosing a totally materialistic or even animalistic lifestyle, to choosing a spiritual one, with all manner of variation in between. The concept of destiny does not make me fatalistic, rather more optimistic, cheerful and serene, due to knowing the true role of the outcome of that destiny. Destiny is my self-responsibility, and what happens is a function of the cosmic laws. Because I believe and feel the central Divinity of the Cosmos, I accept the pain as well as the pleasure of life equally and with equanimity, (because all experience is part of that Divinity).

I made my choices and then sat or fell back unable to process: *Life and the Universe.* My life was unmanageable, and that is when the Divine has come down in the form of grace. And this is spirit guidance. It's a surrender thing! I have realized that the mind's activities are transient and fickle, and the light of yogic awareness burns steadily behind the mental screens. We reach the transcendental through the awareness of the light. Through our deepest subconscious, we can return to our chosen life of being one with Divinity flowing down to all levels of our human endeavor.

The True Self within is so near and yet so hard to

find. All the yogis and gurus, they must recommend you ask the question:

Who am I?

Fear

There is suffering when there is duality.

Where there is another there is fear.

Life is driven by an underlying fear.

Fear of death, of suffering or of life itself, and fear of God.

This is the pain of life the Buddha talked about: "all life is suffering".

Whatever and wherever the journey or pathway to freedom, one thing is clear,

So, life is just a sideshow, which is ultimately totally illusory.

Except for pain!

So it's all Maya! Illusory like a transient dream ending in death.

We need something that works to enable the transcendence of this Maya.

We have to replace it with Truth.

A problem occurs for most of us, because that's not how it works, and that's not how it happens.

If spiritual progress is limited due to limited action, then perhaps only small corners of the darkroom will be lit up. Thus, fear will still be on the agenda. Although it will still have learning purpose. The process is about release, ultimately from all the darkness. Thus, we return in circle to the beginning of the discussion regarding surrender and acceptance.

To worship destruction and darkness in any way seems counterproductive perhaps to the general Western mind. To many in the East, it is very much this God as Destroyer that is sought to gain safety and security. In the Divine Soul, there is no fear, nor any destruction of anything, because fear is just a human creation. This is the outcome of being engaged in in the human condition, and excepting separation from the encompassing universe, whilst not recognizing Divinity. (Either as one Deity or as the impersonal Cosmic Consciousness). To accept & move past fear requires the acceptance of destruction and see its true place in the Cosmic Creation.

Pain and suffering make all the theory irrelevant and can make all our spiritual or religious and therapeutic endeavors almost seem pointless. There is a line of queuing thoughts that like to give fear permission to exist in oneself. However, it's not possible to say fear: "you're out of here". Positive visualizations, however well-meaning, deeming that I am pain-free, just don't work often. Know the type of visualization that already has cognition of ourselves as potentially Divine. Then there is some traction!

Scientists may talk about the function of molecules constantly re-arranging themselves to form things, including humans. Within that concept, see it as a video, film, or play of whatever it is going on, or however you perceive or describe it. It's the process of one's thoughts and understandings about *Life and the Universe.* This includes the thoughts: "I am depressed. I am an addict. "I am a powerful leader", etc. Maybe there should be no problem with just accepting that I am a Divine being really, as why would anyone want all those negative fears, anxieties & doubts? Doesn't make sense! Well possibly it takes time to see it this way and make the necessary corrections.

There needs to be a move past the idea that enlightenment equals: "you are getting what you want, being happy all day and night, and can sort out anything". In Buddhism and Hinduism there are fierce goddesses, depicted in temple icons as cutting off human heads and drinking their blood. Nobody seems to be getting what they want, & yet millions are devotees of the destructive Goddesses, because they do seem to be getting some of what they want. Otherwise, why would they worship that way? There are these forces of destruction that epitomize the nature of this cosmic reality, which in error some religions seek to minimize. "Oh no, our God is not nasty, He's kind and loving". Other religions embrace the Cosmos of Destruction.

Many prefer the more benign & amazing visions, such as of Mary, Mother of God, described as happening in Medjugorje. Or descriptions of someone getting a fantastic vision, being reborn in eureka moments, or having some other transformative experience. To have enlightenment, the dark side must be something understood, and life as it is in its grossness, transcended or transmuted. This is *Alchemy*, as at one and the same time being able to transcend and enjoy the true spiritual meaning of *anything* that lies here and now and beyond. Thus, the chaos makes sense. Thus, the pandemics make sense. Thus, even all the wars of history make sense!

This is also about encountering your true self which

seems covered in fear and the suffering. The human ego is in a position to overcome. Go beyond, though, under. Here lies surrender and acceptance, which is generated through spiritual practice and selfless actions. Knowing the true self would lead also to a space where each moment will bring whatever experience we need when they are needed. (Even the fear loaded ones)! Thus, life as lived, as is also the learning journey, even if there is no spiritual clarity. So, if one cannot understand the purpose of pain, dig a little deeper! Then one can understand, pain, death, world chaos, and drill right down to the minutia of personal life.

Then life is no longer a question! The answers are set up there in what has become instant participation in the vibration of Truth, which illuminates the darkness.

What's my Purpose?

Who am I? What am I? What is my purpose?
What goes on outside, but taken in through our eyes, thoughts, and are senses?
Thought sees "happenings" as something to hold on to and maintain.
More often we see what we want, but we don't get it.

Why do we do what we do?

Why should it work?

However, if that's what works what's wrong with that?

Then all is well also!

It seems that life has a lot of things that we want or positions we want to attain.

By this time, we should not be saying there is anything to fix nor anything to make different!

Perhaps having a purpose is not all it's made out to be.

Certainly, sometimes it seems there is no purpose at all, to anything.

But other times the sun is shining and all is well.

Another time a person may have deep faith Fundamentalist faith can be akin to burying one's head in the sand.

The other prospect is that we get or use what we like and want, and then become addicted to substances or behaviors, which then of course lose their power to pleasure. So perhaps it will be better for all of us, if we just stay out of off the roads! Living out caves and just pass the time. That way we stay out of trouble!

Presumably there is some underlying understanding that answers must come from within us, in order for us to hold the expectation that some form of salvation occurs this way. Indeed, all the teachers in the spiritual sphere will undoubtable mention as some component of their teaching that the Divine is within.

My gurus say that the guru is also actually within. So, some say when you find the Buddha tell him to go away, as you don't then need the guru in human form. In other words, you're done, finished you've got it, and you've got what it needs.
Except this is just the beginning!
Step back & look at the real human needs before jumping into space! (Divine space that is).

In the spiritual world or in the mental health world, there are other things we can do: activities to participate in. At one level there are talking therapies. We can try to heal through counselling or psychoanalytical methods, or with practical efforts, such as using sensory modulation techniques to alleviate anxiety. Physical relaxation methods: practice controlling the breath, listening to soothing music, or practicing some mindfulness type exercise.

If we go further still, then there are other things we may

do. It seems necessary in life to bring in mechanical means to alleviate suffering. An illustration of this is taking medication for physical or mental health problems. We "forcefully" try to resolve the issue. This quite often is reasonably successful, otherwise people would not bother going to doctors or psychiatrists.

We also go into the realm of prayer, using liturgical hymns, or using mantras. Or, on a more physical level, some devotional worship, as for instance performed in temples. We are almost trying to force God to come to the party.

We want to make it happen. Some of it we can touch, talk to, or directly experience through senses, but of course it eventually disappears or vanishes, or changes. Then you need to expose yourself to the Devine Grace through your spiritual practice again and again, until there is no more "again".

And then what life is, still goes on. There is still the mortgage, to pay the pets to feed. Then what is just left is the suffering of the moment, the being in the body here now, which is not really a comfortable place by any measure. The tummy rumbles, the nose itches, it's too hot or too cold, and we are always subject to hunger and thirst, with a need for sleep in a place of safety. Life is pretty dangerous, and it can be extremely dangerous. A matter of just survival for so many billions of people.

So this daily moment to moment practice is what gives us the moment to moment relief, (from our suffering), and this is where we can thrive instead of survive. By this time, we will have formed a connection with our Deity, with our spiritual pathway, and understand the place of our particular religious beliefs in the whole picture.

Chapter 5

Descending grace!

Tara Goddess

We have discussed a lot of issues which may still seem to be going round and round in circles!

I do not practice a wide range of spiritual pathways, even though I am multi faith and have had quite strong connections with a variety of religions and spiritual groups.

I am a follower of the Goddess and I practice kundalini yoga.

I repeat mantras which represent the centers of the body, and also represent certain Goddess forms, (which are not separate from the whole Shakti form).

I repeat mantras to engage in the spiritual path. Also, because of my own personal sense of desperation!

They give me something indescribable but help me clearly to thrive despite a history of monastic reclusiveness, chronic depression, and a somewhat obsessive and addictive type personality.

The bottom line is that I need both my prayer to my Goddess and repetition of mantras for my own sanity.

The Goddess takes various forms, but it is the same Divinity that is also the Cosmic Consciousness. There is no real separation.

Chakras enable the Goddess Shakti, (power), to flow up and down as the Kundalini through each center from the crown of the head to the base of the spine. I have written considerably about this area in my other books.

My inner spirit guide was, I think, a reflection of me in my monastic type of personality. It seemed to sit on my shoulder in a position and presence such that I have some form of "conversation", as and when needed. It seemed a both male & female energy, as a "reflection" of myself, and didn't intervene so much. More being the voice of wise counsel. This is an energy seemingly separate in some way, and it was something I value strongly.

Whether it's real or not, who knows?

For some reason this spirit energy took a bit of a "back seat" as a new energy came to me. This new female energy presented a before my brow area, as the Goddess energy.

I asked her name and it is Tam.

I did not understand until I researched this name.

As well as my described previous devotional practice, because of my engagement in Buddhist type meditation with a group, I am aware of Buddhist Goddesses including *Tara,* the mother Goddess of all the Buddha's.

I did not previously know that her sound representation is *Tam.*

This sounded to me like a *chakra* seed mantra, as all the chakras have seed mantras associated with each center. Those seed mantras are ascending *Lam, Vam, Ram, Yam, Ham, Aum.*

I don't use these mantras for my kundalini or chakra meditation, as I use other seed mantas as described in *Om Divine Grace.* (Relating to specific Goddess forms).
Tam although sounding like another seed sound, is a Divine sound that emanates from the heart of the Goddess Tara.

This is not associated with a chakra center, although after a few days I find that *Tara* seed sound is *Triim.* This I experience as emanating from my heart area. (Slightly to the right and slightly outside the body, but attached)

Tara is another form of the Hindu Goddesses with which I am very familiar but is much more popular in Tibetan Buddhism. So, *Tara* is a Goddess form, which some Tibetan gurus say is to be visualized as standing level with the eyebrows, or the third eye.

The *Tam* sound is to be visualized emanating from the Goddess, who is seated on a Lotus, and takes a beautiful young girl form, colored green. (There are also White, Blue and Red *Taras*).

I am inspired by this Shakti power, whatever form she takes, and hence continue to say, (as in the previous book), my writings are Goddess inspired...........

Now I incorporate some of the seed mantras of *Tara* into my daily practice but have not written about them in depth yet.

I put myself into the stream of the Divine Grace through my spiritual practices, but I try not to expect any specific outcomes. This is the outcome of a lifetime!

My practices over the years since 1966 have been in fruition.

Hence, I write! (Under Inspiration).

Goddess inspired.

It would be nice to live a life that is easy without pain and without fear. Maybe possible for some to some degree. If we read the news, look around us, and possibly look at our own lives, we will see that this is not the case for the vast majority of people for the vast majority of the time.

From a spiritual perspective: *Life and Universe* is a learning experience for every moment or every breath.

Fear is a natural part of life since caveman times, when the fight or flight response was essential for survival. Now fear seems like a substratum, the foundation of our daily lives, and something that's happening all the time, including and up to, the fear of death. We do a lot of things both for our survival and because we are fearful about what might happen to us if we don't do certain things.

The spiritual teachers or Guides tell us that we are Divine beings, and in our Divine consciousness we are naturally free from fear. This does not translate into reality and probably never will if we are honest! Alright, reality itself may be seen as an illusion without permanence, it's a philosophy idea that for most of us, still does not translate into something spiritually meaningful or lived experience.

It will be helpful to be centered and focused within one's heart with solidarity with the level where you find a light that shines and inspires. This is where fear does not exist, and this translates or rather transforms the negative or dark energy in our lives. It will not just go away! It needs to be transmuted as in an alchemical process, and this may not happen in a "flash of light". (As in "I have seen the light"). Anything towards helping us to deal with fears, anxieties and depressions, will also help alleviate our core fear. However, with significant clinical levels of depression/anxiety, medication may have benefits!

Cancer and other physical illnesses also will not just go away, just because we think we will, or may, take them out of existence. Again, there are those who have been "miraculously" cured, and those who have received great medical benefits.

But it is *fantasy thinking* to start putting any kind of

outcomes in place, as the *guaranteed benefit* of any spiritual practice, positive thinking, or therapeutic healing etc. This is all ego territory, and the earnest spiritual practitioner should stay focused on what the real outcome of practice is. (Hopefully better self-surrender, better service of others, and a natural "high" based on love towards all life).

So, when we say, according to the Gnostic type philosophies, that I am the Cosmic Consciousness, or at least a Divine being, we are in psychological terms creating positivity and outlines or sketches for our individual souls to "feel into" the Cosmic Soul. (Who is free from all blemishes, including fear, disease and pain). That is if we don't muddy the waters with our ego expectations.

The purpose or the agenda of the Truth is self-realization, not freedom from being human, or experiencing what it is to be human. Human experience still goes on even for the so-called realized person, because of the cumulative effects of past karma. This experience of remaining in the body and experiencing spiritual resonance with Truth while still having work, family, physical elements, fear and anxiety, is part and parcel of this thing called:

Realistic Realization or Practical Enlightenment.

Accumulated effects and continuing friction from past actions are transmuted by the self-realized soul, who is unafraid, and doesn't worry about anything, because of Being in Truth. (Also, nothing is seen as "real" from a permanency perspective, including the body and mind).

Getting to this position requires usually some additional activities on the spiritual journey, (other than a pure philosophical stance). This is the case to even just enhance the pace of the spiritual journey, or even to ensure the spiritual journey actually has some practical traction. This is where additional support from one's personal Deity comes into play. Religion has benefits for some!

I my case it's the Goddess who is available to smooth this process, and I dedicate this section to Tara the Tibetan Goddess.

This journey can be expedited in a very physical sense. That is to say one's anxieties and fears can be addressed very front on, very much in the moment, by having oneness with the power and the Grace of the Goddess.

(Through prayer and meditation).

Of course, he or she may do it through the Christ, Krishna, Buddha, or other. Your choice!

The point is there is a need for a personal God to assist in the understanding of a Cosmic Divine energy which is beyond all thought and speech. Therefore, it becomes necessary to be really practical, and except the Divine in whatever form or through whatever process that works to free oneself. There can be no space for judgement of anyone, for as you damn others, so that damnation returns to you.

Do unto others as you would do to yourself.
(So simple, but to really do this seems elusive).

We have first to get into a place of seeing, and feeling the essential unity of the universe, and have the tools to be able to do this sort of thing. As simple human beings we may be lost in our addictions, depressions and anxieties. We may need a whole raft of support type activities around us. Along with our "highest point" philosophy and claim of Self Divinity we may even need some medication for whatever ails us!

From a non-dual perspective, the world is an idea, just a result of thought activity, just an illusion with transient nature. You make things how they are by how you think. The human desires then acts, then then achieves, (or fails). In Divinity one does not act and if any actions take place, it is only the qualities of nature moving. These qualities of nature (the *Gunas*), I have already written about. They range from the pure to the filthy, the dark and deprived, to the place of light and selflessness.

So the spiritual journey requires that we don't give away our agenda of humanity, but we do give away the small individual soul. Especially the agenda that is based on darkness. An ego-based darkness which is full of, not just fear and anxiety, but also hatred, self-serving and the historical mankind starting point for: "divide and conquer". (Historically also: "loot, rape and pillage")!

Although the qualities of nature remain in control of the universe, we retain our self-responsibility for self-determination and choice. A choice to be at the highest level of Being, is claimed by the highest level of practicing spiritually. Focused with rigor and honesty, meditating in that state in the form of the form of God "as you understand Him/Her".

Without operating from one's own perceived or actual state of depression, anxiety, fear etc., the spiritual journey becomes truly focused on the attainment of the highest. It's not where you will worry about the mortgage, what the kids are doing, or whether your hair is falling out, (or losing its color). More importantly it's not where you are going to be angry all the time, because things don't work out the way they should.

You become able to accept what is happening with serenity, without losing your ability to change things, and this is where fearlessness comes in, because you're not frightened of outcomes or what people think of you.

You really get the prayer. (Purpose).
"God grant me the serenity to accept the things I cannot change".
Along with the wisdom to change the things you can.
So here is not just a fake wishy-washy think stance. This can be a powerful, possibly very assertive stance when needed, which is delivered without any internal anger, and is driven by courage.

"And the wisdom to know the difference".

We are based in and around the Divine Reality and not in our illusion driven ignorance.

Tam

(Tam is the core "sound" mantra for Tara)

See life and try to feel the oneness with all, even though there are specifics of separation such as work, relationship and living situation.

There always seems to some degree to be fear and anxiety about the specifics of life, regarding what will or won't occur.

However, this emotional and thought train is the minds reactivity that is a residue even when we are in deep meditation.
We cannot stop being ourselves no matter how enlightened we become. Even annoying little habits remain, or harmless ones.

We can, however, mentally receive all of this as just mind and body continuum. It's all quite normal for human beings to be at times fearful or anxious for instance. Even at clinical or pathological levels of say depression or anxiety, it is still only a mental health disorder that can be managed reasonably successfully with the right application and the right resources. "Treatment works". It's statistical otherwise we would not have myriads of services often spending taxpayer's money.

By being focused on one's True Self it becomes entirely possible to limit both the presentation and effects of any psychological distress. The same could be true for physical illnesses with as pain. Disease can again be "re-seen or re-formatted".

Just stably being in the "witness state", changes significantly the impact of any disorder or disease. This witness state has been described in *Vedanta* philosophy as the soul's overview and oversight of all activities in the world of *Maya*. In Buddhism there is also the meditation process which has been popularized in western culture as a mindfulness way that has therapeutic benefit.

All can be changed, because when we recognize our *Strengths* as opposed to our weaknesses we go about life in a very different way. (See also literature on the

Strengths Model in mental health care).

So, we are talking about modifying something, (say reactivity), which is only part one of the spiritual process. The other part is recreating or creating anew. Being significantly in touch with the Transcendental Soul we move out to another world of Being.

Otherwise, we are like clothes stuck in a dryer going round and round, and yes getting pretty dry, but not out on the line in the sun. Swishing around in just recovery and hope.

Not a bad thing but nevertheless not the full ticket! We need to investigate then how we can live *beyond* our fears and anxieties, by remaining in Divine awareness, even in the midst of daily activities.

By going beyond or transcending, we then move into a space of re-creating where we are no longer just recovering or just managing. Various mental health, addictive and psychological issues especially are put on one side, while we get on with our true purpose. (*Realistic Realization or Practical Enlightenment*). This includes the chronic tendency towards fear and reactivity which propels us to behaviors where we seek to self sooth and possibly leads into activities where we descend into substance use, including food. Depression at a clinical level seems to go hand –in-hand at this point.

We have created what is before us per individual, and we suffer per individual as a result. Of course, happiness and pleasure is there, but sometimes we are just wrapped up in either the getting of it, or the wanting, or the holding on. Then if there is an exclusion of a healthy overview, we don't want to know, until perhaps we hit rock bottom. Therefore, there is not much point in talking to those who are not interested in addressing their pain and remain content to seek pleasure only.

Pleasure though, in a spiritual perspective, is no different than pain, and should equally be addressed by the practitioner of a spiritual process or program. This is all filtered down through the self-identifying process leading to realizing the individual self, (the Atman), as being one with the cosmic consciousness, (Brahman).

Additionally, most of us will need some religious or spiritual activities that are more specific and targeted to help with the gross elements of human existence. This is where we have our own set of prayers, chants, mantas, or liturgies.

The path of knowledge, (Gyana), may be too high a road and unrealistic aspiration for some who also need the devotion to a personal God, which is the yoga of devotion, (Bhakti Yoga). Invariably all of us need to engage in some selfless service to others. (Karma Yoga).

Then there is also the "kingly" pathway or Raja Yoga, where mental and physical specific exercises, including meditation and concentration, are engaged in. (To create a deeper state of spiritual awareness or the "trance" like Samadhi).

There is no reason that anyone cannot sit on higher spiritual levels. The choice is there and available when agreed to. However, it will take time for the benefits of any spiritual endeavor to filter down into our daily business and purify the gross elements of our activities. This includes our diet, use of substances or food to self-soothe, and distractions such as media and Internet, used to avoid facing the truth of our existence, with its daily anxiety and fear levels.

There is always the potential for Divine Grace as we seek contact with our Deity or Higher Power. Then our guiding angels, guardian angels, or spirit guides act as aspects of Divinity and move to support us in our endeavors. We may actually see and hear them or feel them. Or more commonly, realize their connections with us in other ways.

Some spiritual practitioners may be intimately connected with their Gods, spirit or forces, whereas others may just have hope that they are out there, or something is out there that will help them in some way.

The true transformation does occur eventually after persistence, and that may include treating the various more overt issues such as significant depression, addictions, and obsessive bad habits. We may also be afflicted with quite severe personality defects such as narcissism, or a tendency to be aggressive and paranoid about everything around us. These "defects of character" all need attention, and that can be done spiritually by prayer etc., but may need more concrete work as well as through therapeutic support and counselling. Psychiatric support does help when it's really indicated!

The transformation occurs when the small ego based self or personality aligns to the Truth which is other than our inherent nature. Not just a change or different person. We want to be a different Being which is our own Divinity, shining through and lighting up our daily business.

I am!
This comes after we ask: Who am I?

We then are able to practice *mindfulness*, be meditative, and be self-aware. We can be in the moment because we are the moment!

Suffering occurs. Yes, that's what we get for being a changeable entity in a changeable world.

But the world and all its mind or body combinations has a substrate under this illusory Maya. This transitory circus show!
This is the unchangeable Soul beyond ego and personality.

When we are hurt enough from the surface business, we go down and dive deeper and deeper, dependent on to how desperate we are. We even become willing to self-surrender to a Higher Power or Deity and give "handing it over" a "whirl over".

We want that energy. That consciousness.

As we go to God & God comes to us

As we claim our true selves, we receive the Grace that hastens the process.

Life then is not a problem. It then is our teacher, our means of liberation, and a source that we can express gratitude for.

No need to justify either your life and its complexity, or your associated search, which sometimes seems to go on in another dimension. A seemingly circular fashion at times, which nevertheless, even if we don't see it, is completely interconnected with our ever-present Divine nature.

The Divine as me is the nicest stance, but this doesn't mean we are special!

It's only if we can see and pay homage to the Divine in the other person.

Is this realistic?

Is this realistic given we tend to be reactive in

relationships?

Probably relationships are the number one minefield, as far as our emotions and serenity management is concerned.

However, the position of seeing the Divine as already manifest is true, because it is what really already exists. We may seem to be creating a new way of living with a spiritual vision and processes, whereas in fact we are going nowhere in a journey because we are not even on one. (From a higher philosophical perspective of course). More likely we are choosing to accept the Truth but allow it to have overarching Dominion only to the degree that we let it be so.

And this is not surrender!

We may put out our individuated sense of divine consciousness to request that we get assistance in the work of overcoming the small ego base personality.

Of course we fear letting go, and it is this fear that actually prevents us from letting go.

It seems that the fear is based on this: "oh dear I will have nothing left and I will cease to exist".

However, it's true that some personality will remain, even if you become the new Buddha or a big Guru. Also

100

humans by nature have a flight or fight automatic response, which means that some degree of fear and reactivity also remain.

It's all in our nature to be fearful, anxious, and reactive.

And it's in our nature to retain petty defects, such as picking one's nose in public!

The spiritual pathway or journey is more than about being in recovery, even though that person seeks "healing" from the past.

Of course we all want perfect cures, with perfect release from what ails us.

Therefore, the therapeutic or self-help managed interventions will have limitations, which is not to say they won't work very well, especially in terms of recovery or remission.

The true spiritual path goes however, into the transcendental, and sees recovery and remission as almost incidental. This is when we move into a new way of living in a new home for our soul and enter into the Higher Rooms of existence.

This is when we bring the Divine Light into our darkness, or we walk into the light and therefore leave the darkness behind.

Then perhaps, probably, we hope, we leave behind our negative personalities, or rather all the unhelpful mechanisms in our lives, keeping what's essential for physical well-being. This includes keeping those ingrained petty habits that run their own show. (As long as they do no harm).

We no longer label ourselves with dysfunctions we got from our psychiatrists, therapists and spouses. We are not called depressed, alcoholic, borderline, narcissistic or neurotic.

We also move past the need for PTSD, addiction and so forth, simply because we leave the past behind and enter the future of Divine Sanity

Doing this requires a leap. Add on also a choice to make the leap, and to stay with the pathway chosen to Spiritual Nirvana. Even with this choice, healthy action can be difficult within the turmoil of everyday life, which does not want to let go. Even the monks and the nuns get this problem! That's why we have a Deity, a Higher Powers, Incarnations or even God. (Preferably a Goddess)!

They are there to help us to be present, by them being present in our lives

We are then truly in the moment

Some have angels, some get transmissions, some get channeling

In the pathway enumerated in previous writings there is Kundalini Yoga. In this line of practice, we attain the realization which in Sanskrit is called *Sākshāt.* We get a *Samādhi* which is *Saguna.* Sa meaning "with", and *Guna* meaning the quality or form. Without form is *Nirguna,* where *Nir* means "without". Those who seek the path of knowledge or *Gyāna*, will seek the *Nirguna* and those who need or want a personal God stay with the *Saguna.*

It matters not if the realization is of the Personal Divine or Cosmic Consciousness.

However, the transcendent impersonal form realization is historically considered difficult for "ordinary" humans to attain. It seems to be a domain of rigorous reclusive introspection or renunciation, such as obtained by monks, nuns and saffron-robed yogis who meditate all day, based in monasteries and caves.

However now there is transformation for our age, and it is within.

Therefore, it does not really need the external cave dwelling or robes. Boots, shoes, suits or T-shirts will do!

More importantly it's not about changing jobs, marriage, and relationships.

Especially the relationships!

Seeking comfort is a distraction from the real work of overcoming fear and reactivity, let alone desire. However, we are in situations where we need to be. This is at any given time, if we can accept, it learn from it, and transcend it.

If we fight the dream, the illusion or impermanence, we support it in some ways. If we bring it into the light of Truth the darkness disappears along with the "crazy dream".

We are free, not only from our need for salvation, but from the journey also.

We are already where we want to go!

Chapter 6

Paramhansa Ganesh Giri

Ganesh Giri is my name as a swami, or holy-man. This was the name I used in India and that time is written about in my previous books.

I have learnt that I don't need to justify why I would want to be in a certain spiritual space with a certain spiritual identity

That identity is both enmeshed in my reality as an English man called Raymond and as a monk in India.

I am trending towards identifying again with the holy man persona at this time, because I'm seeing more and more that we are all Divine as well as human. Why not also have a spiritual name?

I just had a long run of forty plus years in the Western world with an identity mostly as a "European New Zealander", (as per the cultural line in the census forms).

Also after all, Ganesh Giri only got a few years of use! So, this is a claim of independence based on my search for release from all the attachments.

These attachments do not go away except that in the holy man identity they are covered over by the light of Truth, whereas in the Englishman identity the Light is covered over by the attachments.

This dual identity seems to me to be a better deal and idea for the future or in the long run.

I like the idea of a heavenly kingdom even if it's not somewhere I recognize easily, as long as I feel it's more present and attainable in the moment to moment.

This is identity made at a higher level as something that I am party to by Divine Grace coming down into my life, as I rise up to the Higher Rooms through self-surrender.

This is a wonderful creation then, where the Cosmic Conscious can then fully manifest in me through the grace of the Divine Goddess

My tendency as a human has been to throw it away and replace it with trash!

The *Giri* part of my name means "mountain". This is the place where I am sitting wherever the body is and represents my journey. (As in going up the mountain).

And in this identity, I am on the peak, and look down on my small ego personality

Even so at times the surroundings seem precarious

and steep.

Luckily as a Capricorn I have am also a mountain goat and thus well equipped for the terrain!

Perhaps this was a design from my Deity to me as my birthday gift.

I feel safe, but knowing that if I do go back down, I go back into my fears, anxieties and depressions.

Or worse maybe?

The days of should and must seem to be below the clouds which shroud the lower slopes.

Historical data leads to historical expectations, but I need to refrain from probing more than one day at a time. The historical future is the hysterical future!

No more prescriptions for life let alone for medication. The new life is not a new consciousness but rather an acceptance of consciousness as it really is.

Acceptance of myself as it really should be, as one investing in Truth.

Is this not freedom?

As it is about being and not doing, I am released from the need to prove that I am indeed a *Giri*, the mountain man or rather the *Giribaba* as the "old" wise man on the mountain.

I don't need to sit there cross-legged in ochre robes

because the first part of my given name from my holy man days is *Ganesh*.

Previous writings have talked about *Gunas*, the qualities of nature, and *Ganesh* simply means Lord of the *Gunas*, (thus implying control over the human nature of life).

As it is the qualities of nature that function in all life at all times, those qualities nevertheless do not impinge on the True Self of consciousness, which is transcendental.

Consciousness is the witness of all, and all means *whatever* we are up to.

This could mean technically, theoretically, that it is ok to indulge in less than pure activities.

I know though that the ego personality with the defects of character wants to remain wallowing in addiction, depression anxiety and fear, which are engendered by live with the darker qualities for nature. (Tamasic and Rajasic).

All the things that bring fun and enjoyment are not necessarily benefiting any of us.

Nevertheless, we can't and we don't want to be living a boring colorless life with no fun.

Therefore, the spiritual changes occurring must be

naturally easy and be what is desired, (if those changes are to stick).

This is why it's easier to wander along the flat then to start climbing up a mountain

It's hard work going up the slopes and the further up we get away from civilization the less amenities we find.

In India some of the yogis I found on mountains lived a very sparse life.

They may have had tea leaves, and collected water from springs

But if you want milk in your tea you're out of luck.

Don't even ask for a cappuccino!

Divine grace again!

So, there is some renunciation or giving up but again it has to be by choice, and something that comes natural and it fairly easily until it becomes ingrained,
Yes, we think that we need this or that to be safe, or to be functional, and yes, we will probably be saying this even when we're on the peak of the mountain.
Perhaps this is why even angels sometimes fall from grace!

The thing to remember is that living at a higher level and in a higher vibration brings its own fun. Its own bliss
Its own sanity, and its own peace
Having imbibed of this enough one will forget about the lower pleasures, or they will seek to cease to be so desirable or cease to command so much attention.
The robes will not be ochre, but they will be new garments, and the old garments of fear will be thrown aside.

The light of truth makes this transformation and when the going seems too tough, then and often then, we begin to perceive the flow of Divine Grace.

The Divine Grace lift this up and completes our journey for us when we are unable to do so. We live with the illusion of freedom and believe that we have to do certain things to make sure we have enough to eat and to survive.
We all have debts, of some sort, but running from our previous experiences will make sure exhaustion, (of running away), leads to more exhaustion

This is why some scriptures talk about redemption and being lifted up. This however occurs when there is surrender, and when there is choice to know one's True Self, accompanied by a willingness to act to make this so. As I write now in my 70's I can look at my wrinkles, I can experience more tiredness and wonder about all I have done or rather not done.

However, the Divine Grace has remained, and I can understand myself as beyond all of this. Certainly, I can understand my identity as the "lord of the qualities of nature who lives as the mountain man". Added to that is not the prefix or title of swami, but *Paramahansa.* A great swan!

(Just as the swan floats on water so the *Paramhansa* floats on *Samsara*,* without getting "wet"). Add to that the mountain goat, that is the Capricorn.

** Samsara* (a Sanskrit word literally meaning "continuous flow") is the repeating cycle of birth, life, death and rebirth (reincarnation) within Hinduism, Buddhism, Bön and Jainism.

So, I feel justified in being joyful and thankful and grateful!

Belief

The Deity or God/Goddess is beyond description but could be seen as the totality of all and thus is "perfect or complete". This creation and the creator and are then Whatever: *Life and the Universe.*

This phenomenal world can then be seen as perfect for our requirements whether that is to enjoy, ("eat, drink and be merry"), or to do penance in caves, and return to out Divine state.

Incidentally we are already Divine, but are enveloped in the illusory powers of *Maya,* and thus think we are body/mind, personality and ego.
We are perfect and complete as we are.

Whatever is produced of the Cosmic Consciousness cannot be a duality of good and evil. Or enjoyment and pain cannot be different! (This is "advanced consciousness").
The whole is complete in itself. But the universe emanates from Him, (or Her).

Everything must then be in complete balance. Even when

that balance is chaos, pandemics, wars and planet loss. (As happens apparently at the end of this era known as *Kali Yuga*).

Everything animate or inanimate that is within the universe is controlled and owned by the one Deity. This is because ones Deity varies. It can be inside of a religion or as a Higher Power or something else.

We all choose something different as per our culture, religion or belief system. We all possible differ even if slightly on an individual basis when it comes to our perception of, say, the Buddha or the Christ. (Even if we are in the same "subset", of Catholicism or Tibetan Buddhism etc.)

One should be happy therefore to accept only those things necessary for life, but of course we all want for ME. We have a quota, as our lot in life, because we are sustained by life itself, which is of course Divine. Our delusion within consciousness identifies via our ego/personality with the external worlds and sees our wants and desires as of primary importance.

This then leads to the illusion of not having enough, not

being good enough, and in its extremities may lead to self-harm and suicidal thoughts! Matter is impermanent, since it is created in birth and destroyed in death. The external world ages and changes. Your house will be gone in a thousand years!

This process, including death, or loss, usually gives rise to fear, and we want to "get stuff fast", as we don't understand the real issues nor ask the right questions.
Who am I?
What am I?
What is my real purpose?

If you're happy with that, throw this book away!
We usually don't know who we are. Because we don't pursue questions related to meaning and consciousness. We ignore them, for logical and very human reasons. Too scary!
We want to control nature also.

It's scary because we then have to confront the facts that all is just momentary, and pleasure, drugs, alcohol, sex are not a permanent solution to birth, old age, death and disease.

Surrender seems like loss of all, but acceptance allows for real freedom from fear. You find out who you really are and what the world really is.

The world has been here for a long, long time. Don't worry about it. Worry about your identity and the basic questions of existence: What is reality? What is experience? Who is experiencing? These spiritual questions can take you to a blissful alternative.
Whatever you do will garner learning
Culminating into knowledge, eventually.
Acceptance requires that you lose your ego/personality.
Except the useful bits!
There is nothing like a suitable Mantra, to "shortcut" the whole process.

Usually that means guidance, and possibly a living Guru. We all are a collective and individual consciousness simultaneously. We are all seeking true pleasure.

We all are seeking the ultimate truth. We all are seeking immortality, an end to all misery/nothingness.
Mantra - it is a combination of special sounds and vibrations that purify space, body, mind and consciousness from negative energies. Mantra – it is an

ancient sacred formula that gives a powerful Divine energy, and it is the key that opens the way to the Supreme Divine knowledge. Repeat the mantras as much as possible.

A Rosary also helps with concentration on the mantra and meanings, for the beginner.
Again, get advice on this from somewhere (The Internet is better than nothing)!
It comes down to this:
Who am I?
What am I?
What is my role in life now?

Hari Om Tat Sat

Chapter 7
Spiritual Practice

Depression, Addiction, and Spirituality

Spiritual people may struggle with different types of addiction. They may experience depression. (Some more severe than others). One of the most interesting aspects is the recognition that prior or within the depression, most of them were rather disciplined, in control of things and life events, and even "succeeding". This is also a reminder to me that before & during my own experience, I was often optimistic with a strong sense of accomplishment. I believed in my ability to achieve, but when in significant depression, it was very difficult to keep this sense within me.

Is it possible that the initial cause of depression in the first place has to do with a very high expectation for oneself? The expectations that may be imposed externally about being spiritually "good" or being "perfect in God's presence". Spirituality seems to be about finding the essential self within - the presence of God. The only way to come to God though seems to become the way we essentially are. If we are anything else, we will only end up dishonoring God. Spirituality is God's invitation to us in all aspects of who we are. Spirituality is that space that allows us to just be and be ok with who we are. It negates any attempt to be what society wants us to be. It negates any attempt to find the high in spiritual experience. It "is what it is." It is not going out looking for God and proving yourself to God. It is in knowing that God is in the very *"isness"* of us.

This leads to a question. Is it possible that certain understandings of spirituality can lead to depression &/or addiction and not the other way around? Personally, while I see that it is possible that pondering spiritual ideas can lead to depression, it is equally possible that the opposite is true. "Depression experience" can also be a central part of the spiritual path. Some say we must go through a Dark Night of the Soul to attain spiritual growth, & that it is wrong to see depression as somehow negating our spiritual growth. "Happy times" are not necessarily the most growth producing.

I led a very disciplined life as a monk in my twenties but have since found that depression caused more changes in my actual behavior than disciplined spiritual practice ever did. It seems that what we become as a result of facing the dark times is the transformed soul. Perhaps "normal" people can go about their lives pretending everything is fine, but we can't. We are faced with conditions or disorders that grab our attention and will kill us if we do not take action and turn it into our advantage. Seeing the advantage can give you the insight to use every tool at your disposal to turn your "curse" to benefit.

Spirituality is a topic of increasing interest to clinicians, but there is a diversity and lack of clarity of understanding. Conceptual components of spirituality include "relatedness, transcendence, meaning/purpose, wholeness, and consciousness". This is in opposition to "moroseness, uselessness, lack of energy, inability to sleep, and a poor attitude toward life in general". (Among other symptoms of depression).

According to recent statistics, depression, is practically an epidemic, with over 70 million people suffering from its effects. Thus, we want more spirituality & less depression. More happiness, ingenuity, energy, and ability to reach a higher potential in life.

Some very talented people struggle with different types of depression &/or addiction. Some committed churchgoers or practitioners of other religions and even monks or priests struggle also. Generally, it's hard to tell whether depression comes first or it's the addictive/obsessional behaviours. So sometimes a person who is very capable, organised and has a strong sense of morality may succumb to addiction as well as depression. There is a view that oversensitive persons, who seek perfection in many areas, may be easily subject to negative moods when they believe they haven't performed or achieved whatever it is they are supposed to.

It can be worse for someone who believes they have found some source of mystical belief and has had an experience of God or a Higher Power. Then addiction and depression can feel like, or seem like, a fall from grace. This is an idea or belief itself which can compound the problem. In another perspective we could say that addictions or depression may drive the search for truth and sanity, and lead to spiritual practice or religious participation. Some religions say that we will become perfected beings, (eventually!). Whoever is writing or whatever the scripture, there seems to be an exhortation to hold onto faith, as that will lead us onwards and upwards and out of our mess. Whether that's true or not is something else! Faith may just be a support to hang onto, and spirituality may be a hope giver and purpose or context provider.

There is an issue about the difference between religion and spirituality, and whether one or the other is more likely to help cure, or from another opposite perspective, to cause problems.

In depression there is poverty of mood & the lure of something which gives a mood burst is very tempting. Nobody wants to feel dead even if in the depression one can want to be that. The addict gets momentarily times of feeling not just alive but super alive, only to plunge down in the comedown. In addictions at some point there can be moments when one feels the presence of a higher reality, and then there is some hope. When this is truly felt there is an immediate sense of relief, albeit temporarily. It may be then that dark sadness heralds a drive to find meaning to go past the sense of loss of pleasure, disenchantment and avoidance of activities of life.

Even for a health professionals the whole area of spirituality and religion may seem to be a somewhat empty vista, even a foreboding or forbidden territory. We have to wonder why this is and what it is that affects even health professionals and may even causes us to skirt around this territory. One can come up with a lot of reasons of course. Look at the history of religion and the pain it caused. Look at spirituality focused practices and see how fundamentalist some people have become, even without a mainstream religion. So, the search for meaning in life could be associated with a higher degree of malady. The keyword here though is - associated. It seems one has to find one's own meaning in this paradox.

There sometimes seems to be no reason to be here apart from getting brief periods of pleasure artificially. Therefore, having a purpose and reason to be here is a protective factor, and it may help considerably in prevention of self-harm and suicide. Religious and spiritual treatises tell us that we will achieve afterlife as a result of healthy activities, and that deliberate termination of life may cause problems with these processes. As a result of suicide, we might not go to heaven. Or if we believe in future lifetimes and rebirth, we may have to come back to start the whole process over again and re-experience our problems. There is also the issue of what we are thinking about at the time of death. If this is dark black material thought processes, we may find ourselves in a dark black space.

Why do people on their deathbed suddenly feel the fear of God, suddenly see the light, and get the blessings? The spiritual teachers exhort us to turn to our Lord, our Divinity, and take up some meditation practice or worship and pray. The power of the Divine Name is much vaunted as is self-surrender and faith that your guide will always present you with the requisite guidance.

Problems themselves in life do sometimes seem to have a purpose. If we live long enough to look back over lengthy periods, we may say, "well that caused me a lot of pain and I've learnt so much more. I became so much stronger & more capable". There is always a test when going through difficulties, sufferings or just daily business. There does however seem to be a purpose, just as in going to school as a child gets more ready for life and learns perspective as well as knowledge. All the other growing up things that we experience make us into a "well adjusted" adult. One hopes!

Happiness and *"Truth-Knowledge-Bliss"*

Why do we want to be happy? Does everyone want to be happy? Such questions seem to remain un-answered for ever. Nobody can hope to fully & scientifically analyse the state of mental happiness, nor explain easily why it is so important to us. What we can do however is to sidestep the theorising and practice of trying to define the intangible and look at our wants in a realistic manner. We can and should get the most out of our lives, but not necessarily by any particular attainment. It seems a fallacy that success & happiness, (call it what you will), is to be *achieved,* if we believe that a state of perfection is no further than our true innermost self. Yet we do not see, except or recognise it, (this natural s innermost self), easily. Why?

If we are really perfected souls, why then are we very imperfect? What can be more perfect in so many ways than the amazing facts of human life and the world and cosmos around us? So brilliantly designed and conceived and yet seen as so flawed in so many respects!

To answer our questions and realise a truth that is already there, we have to seek guidance usually. It is as if we are blind, and yet with help can reach a place where our eyes will be opened and we will see the truth of what has been described to us. In some ways it does not matter who guides us really or which path we take, as in time we will the probably find our own way. It is a matter of making the journey to start with, setting out and having a desire to be in a different, illuminated state of self-knowledge.

The word *self-knowledge* is a useful term to describe or mean the state that a seeker of happiness should attain. This ties in with an interest in a chosen spiritual philosophy that can be used as the core of the search to achieve and understand intellectual and spiritual goals. One such path or philosophy that we can draw on as a particular source for inspiration is *Vedanta*. (There are lots of books on this topic). In the eyes of the Western world, Vedanta seems to be part of Hindu philosophy, albeit at the extreme end of the scale, as it seems to present a somewhat strictly monotheistic view. (And a monastically inclined one). It can be seen however as a universal expression of spiritual truths. In Vedanta the "apparent" world is *Maya*. We could say "unreal", although in slang that means "fantastic". We actually mean false or fake, in comparison to the essential Divine nature of the universe, which is *Anirvachaniya,* or a reality which "words & thoughts cannot reach".

How real is the body? It dies and then does not exist. How real is a dream? It ends and then does not exist. Where then one might ask has the real world been hidden? When we dream, we exist within a world that is very real to us at that moment, and the outside world is blocked out by sleeping mental and physical faculties. Life still exists, not really as a hidden world at all, as we know that the world around us goes on even when we sleep. We know this however by intellectual knowledge, not necessarily by any direct awareness that functions during our sleep. When we wake up from a weird dream, we know that the strange people and places we experienced were false reality. Yet we still feel a chill and awaking has not distanced us completely from our imaginings or dreaming.

If we walk out in the dark and see in the gloom something lying on the path in front of us we hesitate. Is it a snake? It may be just a piece of thick rope which appears in the gloom to be a snake. We are momentarily frightened until our eyes adjust to the object and we laugh inside at our silliness. In the murkiness of our minds we erroneously perceive the world about us to be something other than it really is. When we are very young, we believe that the height of affluence is to possess a bag of sweets or a posh doll, a new cricket bat or a modern bicycle. Adults may laugh at childish naiveté yet see nothing about their own desires for a turbo model car or the latest in lounge furniture. No doubt someone in the heavens is looking down with amusement on the childish fantasies of fully grown adults, and yet we take ourselves seriously whether as children or senior citizens.

All our games are usually played as real, and we do not want to be put down as daydreamers. Not until perhaps our last days when, as we know, there are quite a few conversions to some religion or philosophy on the deathbed. When we are about to depart this mortal world our prowess in chess or in sports, or on the stock exchange becomes a non-entity. People can remember us for our achievements when we are gone, but do we actually get to enjoy adulation as if we were alive and there?

Where is then the way to real happiness? Do we avoid the world completely because it is like passing dream? We cannot usually spend the whole time in trance, nor even alcoholic stupor or drugged euphoria. The reality of our continuous dream of life impinges upon our consciousness to a greater or lesser extent, whether we choose or not. We are bound by our bodies, upbringing and personal environment to live out our lives as long as we live. There is no simple escapist route that avoids the facts of life and death. Happiness then it anywhere and must live within our own experience, if it lies anywhere, or if it exists at all even.

Perhaps before we start spending any more of our time on the pursuit of happiness we should consider whether or not we are really wasting our efforts. We know due to universal experience that some states have an utter inner peace and tranquillity and do exist even when we are in deep sleep. We can experience deep and profound rest from our problems and woes, and we know this because when we are awake, we say to ourselves that we had a wonderfully refreshing rest. If we are in pain and receive some injection that works, we can go into the state bordering on euphoria because of the effect of the drug, and also the release from an immediate and urgent physical pain. It's such a relief. On a more mundane level we might jump for joy when after days or weeks of some hassle or problem, and we have a breakthrough or a change of luck perhaps. Note that often the arousal of happiness is almost dependent on some previous misery, tiredness or trouble. Happiness is achievable but may also be transient and the result of having an opposing unhappy time!

True happiness is not something achieved by a change of our mood in reference to our surroundings. True happiness is a natural state, unaffected by a good or bad luck, by tiredness, sleep, or by our pain or euphoria. True happiness is not even happiness at all; it is something else described in other words. Unfortunately, we do not seem to have very suitable word or words in English language that properly refers to this state of being - that is not the result of external or mental influences. There is however in Sanskrit a very interesting phrase - *Sat, Chit, Ananda.* This phrase describes the state which is the very innermost nature of all life on earth and elsewhere. *Sat* means the Truth. *Chit* means Consciousness, and *Ananda* means Bliss. This is the description of the unchangeable inner soul, as well is that for the Divine cosmic presence. Truth-Knowledge-Bliss.

The way to our inner self is by negating or removing all the fluctuating and transient and moods that range from abject misery to wild euphoria. To do this we need some mechanism by which we can purify or still the fluctuating mental waves that wash hither & thither within our skull, like water in a bathtub. Note that we may not be able to subtract much from our thought patterns. We cannot just dump our mental processes, because there is no way of just removing them - except by dying, and there is nowhere else to put them. We do not need an extractor mechanism, we need something that will calm the turbulent emotions of grief and anger, elation and confusion, and allow the mind to become calm clear lake in which we can experience the reflected joy of our inner soul, and the Sat, Chit, Ananda of the Divine.

What is?

Vedanta: Means literally end of the *Vedas* and is a part of the vastness of Hindu philosophy. Vedanta however, on the surface, seems to oppose the Vedic & Hindu religion in a major way and on major points, and separates away from the concept of worshipping many gods or performing rituals. God is one transcendental state, without specifically denying the value and purpose of a personal god. It does critically analyse Vedic sacrifice and worship of the various deities, and even penance of the yogis.

Vedanta seeks to clear away the clutter of ritual, and point to the discovery of the inner soul, the *Atma*, which is one with the cosmic soul, *Brahma*. Vedanta is not the pathway of devotion to a Personal God. It is a way of being already perfected souls in oneness with the whole of creation. It may be hard to swallow, that we ourselves are God, as the Atma is the same substance as Brahma. The Vedantic mantra is *Tat Twam Asmi* – That I Am. Or the mantra, *Soham* – I am that (Brahma), meditated on with the inhalations and exhalations of breath. I am Brahma, Cosmic Consciousness

Kundalini: Otherwise known as the serpent power, which is considered to be like a coiled snake of energy at the base of the spine. It can be coiled there in a dormant state & when awakened the energy or *Shakti* arises in a sinuous movement through the centre of the spine to the crown of the head. Along the way are centres of energy called *chakras* and each one of those chakras has specific and particular attributes.

Shakti: Considered to be the universal energy or Goddess energy - the creation force of the divine being. In this sense the masculine aspect of divine being is seen as a transcendental power which is beyond form and shape & the female aspect is seen as the external creation. When practitioners worship the Shakti or Goddess form they can worship the divine being as the world, the universe, or creation.

Mantra*:* Is a Sanskrit word. The first part of the word means "constant thinking of" The second part of the word means "that by which one is protected."

So, by the conscience thinking of a certain word one is "protected', where the word protection has a wider connotation in spiritual terms, as being a means to a degree of perfection (*siddhi*). The part *Man* means literally to think and the word *Tra* means literally to protect or free. The repetition or use of a mantra is considered to be enabling of a range of outcomes, from enlightenment down to the acquisition of wealth and pleasure.

The repetition of a mantra is called *Japa*. In Hinduism it is said in Scriptures that in this age, the Dark Age, (*Kali Yuga*), that the repetition of certain mantras is the easiest way to obtain enlightenment. However, there may not seem to be much science or evidence associated with such a view.

Chakra: In Sanskrit, chakra translates into "wheel". These "wheels" can be thought of as vortexes that both receive & radiate energy. There are seven major energy centres or chakras, in the human body. They run from the base of the spine to the crown of the head. Emotions, physical health, & mental clarity affect how well each chakra can filter energy. This in turn dictates how pure the energy is that's emitted from different regions of the body.

Chapter 8

Calming the mind

The Indian sages used a method called yoga, (meaning to yoke), and meditated on a light in the heart or used a hypnotic mantra. Mantra is a word or sound which is supposed to have real and direct junction with its sacred meaning. In all religions we find that there is some symbol or word usage that is used for the purpose of concentrating the mind, channelling it towards Divinity. Verbal formulae however is used also in witchcraft, primitive ritual and even the repetitive lines that we used to get as children in school when we got detention. It is not so much a question of the word sound or sentence itself, but rather the repetition that is intended to concentrate the mind.

Repetition is a rather negative way to go about achieving some degree of one pointed concentration, as it then becomes a matter of blocking thoughts. When we study or watch a good film or some sport, we have focused the mind and blocked the world and its problems outside. When we come out of the film into the cold night air, for all the distraction that the film engendered we return to the same world.

That is not to say that the value of mantra as repetitive practice is a negative means to achieving either mental tranquillity or happiness. The point is that the real permanent and changed happiness (with a capital H), is something else - a separate entity. It is a natural achievable entity but unfortunately sometimes seems to lie at the heart of a maze. Just as a person with a map can find a route through a strange city, so if we are equipped with a map of the workings and ways of the subtle mental forces behind a world existence, we can plot our way to the heart of reality. We need to know what the mind is, what it does and how it functions. We need to know the effect of our mind on our lives, our personalities, and most importantly on happiness. We need to know how other minds affect ours, and understand national minds, and culture.

If the information that we need for our map is beginning to sound a bit complex don't worry. Even in a big city like London if we wish to reach the centre we only need to approach from one direction, as we only need one route in order to reach a goal. Similarly, if we wish to weave our way through the minds maze and hit the centre, we only need some fairly simple instructions of and knowledge of what we are likely to encounter on the way - the landmarks as it were.

It is easier if you have a space in which to think and reflect in peace and quiet. You therefore set aside time for your purpose in this matter, leaving family friends and business to wait a while, making the spiritual journey a very important part of your life. Unlike money in the bank this is practice that you can take with you to the beyond, so, sit on your own and reflect or meditate, whether it be everyday week or month. Without these recharging interludes, our human spiritual batteries run flat, and sometimes we even become incapable of resolving simple ordinary life conflicts, let alone deep meaning full ones. Taking out your own time and space is not antisocial; it allows you to develop into a better person all round.

Many perceive that withdrawal from social activities is only negative, but "non-activities" are not destructive. It is the very nature of the world that it throws up to each individual "waiting periods". It is a natural protective phenomenon even when nothing seems to be happening and even if we feel frustrated, agitated, or bored when we cannot be getting on with something. If we can imitate nature's own method, and create our own quite uneventful periods, we control better our destiny and future. (Instead of being like a leaf that is blown hither and thither by events and people around us). There are a variety of phenomena that are sometimes placed upon us by circumstance, and free seemingly empty time may not be an easily acceptable space, simply because of how we may perceive it.

It is also something of a shock that having sat down, having cleared a space, and started meditating, that agitation, boredom etc. may arise and dominate the mind. This meditative space can be a wonderful and necessary refuge but may also stir a variety of unwelcome thoughts that had not been in the plan. This may be why we don't hear much public eulogy about the benefit of meditation, because it is a common experience that sitting down even to 5 or 10 minutes in absolute stillness can be akin to herding cats! The mind is a wild untamed creature for many, which leads rather than is lead. When you decide to do something about this and have a disciplined state of affairs, the mind (or perhaps rather the ego), can become most upset and tries to resist attempts at any form of mental introspection. Meditation can be difficult and even "depressing" - that is just the first obstacle!

To overcome the fickle mind is not easy and it may seem impossible to get to a state of perfect yoga. A perfect yogi is not one who can sit in a cave motionless in months at a time. If one controls his or her mental environment wherever that may be, the setting is not so important. However, environment can play a large part in any yogic practice as suitable surroundings, access to guides, and spiritual information, may help aid the mental processes. We can only do so much and only afford so much of our time getting into mental shape, but we cannot mend perfectly a pot that is broken and from which there are a few pieces permanently missing. We do what we can in this respect, just like bringing an older car up to a state of roadworthiness by fine tuning and renovation.

When we practice yoga for our physical well-being it is called *hattha yoga*. This is a system of exercise, not just to make a fit and healthy body, but to assist in purifying our mind. Purification of the body means that even the subtle and microscopic parts of the nervous system are cleansed, paving the way for higher mental-based exercises. Such exercises lead then from action or *Kriya* yoga to *Raja* or "Kingly" yoga path, where we move on then to meditation via specific exercises and perhaps use of mantras. Sounds or words associated with inward spiritual states require time to practice to achieve perfection or attainment, called *Siddhi*, in sufficient depth. This may seem difficult as most of us cannot aspire to the heights of ascetics who live in caves and meditate all their waking hours. However, mantra meditation, once set into solid rhythm and practice, can be made into an effortless aspect, as then it can be done whilst doing other activities at any time. We need something that doesn't need us to dip into our precious time and enables us to boost mood to something better than bearable. We need to be able to transcend our daily problems at times without having to put ourselves into a trance like state of mind.

Advaita Vedanta, or "without duality" is not the pathway of devotion to a Personal God. The very form or substance of life *is* Sat-Chit-Ananda, or Existence-Consciousness-Bliss. All that Vedanta treatises teach can seem a far cry from the world of organised religion, messiahs, bishops and infallible preachers. Advaita Vedanta is almost a "godless" philosophy, almost an atheistic philosophy in some ways. It is a way to realisation as understanding of us and the world as it really is, free from any supernatural power or need for religious belief. Broadly speaking it is not even a Hindu only philosophy, as it is a universal creed that owes allegiance to no religious persuasion.

Many books have been written about the subject in depth and all the Vedantic scripture has been the subject of exhaustive and numerous commentaries by a variety of learned scholars, both Eastern and Western, both ancient and present. You can obtain enough books and information about the subject to last you a lifetime's reading. The problem though, is the application of this concept of being God, or even Godlike, or even of the same substance as God. It is difficult especially when we are tied up with work, marriage and business. When we are tied up with the world of Maya (illusory nature), it can be difficult to really believe that we as individuals are nothing but pure consciousness which has taken various transient human forms within this mire of externalised experience.

When we struggle with depression or addictions or other issues is can seem "mission impossible" to even get a foothold in the spiritual dimension.

To repeat the mantra *Soham* we are saying "I am identical with all the pervasive external and internal life force", and we are practising a philosophy that says don't identify yourself with body or mind, or with your role in the day ahead. It's a simple deep breathing, with mantra in tune with the essence of self, which will help you to float through the day in serenity. It is useful to wake up 5 to 10 minutes before you need to do anything and use that short space of time in vital introspection. You need to make your day goes smoothly, so give yourself time to reflect, and try to visualise the individual power of being merged into the big wide Universe.

Breathe Soham to surrender your day into the Divine aspect of the forces which control the circumstances you are to encounter. You cannot avoid some trying circumstances ahead of you, although you plan or program to do this, and try to have a large say in the proceedings. Worrying will not necessarily change things for the better but learning to relax and be meditative allows you to flow with events that you're unable to control, and you may find yourself doing things more easily and more smoothly than you've even planned! A clear mind is always beneficial in any circumstance and will often help you to come up with the right answer to problems.

The external world - the natural world - can be called seen as energy or Shakti, which is the goddess or feminine form of Creation. Creation as in contrast to the transcendental form of "masculine" energy, but it doesn't have to be seen as separate, nor Atman as separate from Shakti. Taking this further all the processes of life can be seen as being part and parcel of our soul work, and we can then also look at meditating a Trinity of Brahman, Shakti, and Atman. The knowledge of our world, and being able to manage work, money and relationships will also enable us to have a stronger hold on spiritual practice. When we are moving more towards or "expanding" our practice to overtly manage our world for both material and spiritual benefit, we are practicing *Tantra*, as Tantra means "to expand out". (Nothing to do with sex!).

Work for most of us is a perfectly natural function as we are guided by a natural qualities and abilities into doing tasks for which we are most suited. It may seem that we often find ourselves doing something we neither wish to do nor are suited to do, but if we can allow our natural destiny and intrinsic divine nature to predominate, we can move into different spaces of allowing ourselves to find our natural work position. Seen in this light a soldier who fights because he born a warrior type personality, is simply fulfilling his destiny, even though his work may involve killing other humans! He is complying with a subtle set of universal laws that govern all out work.

Such ideas may not appeal to a pacifist and those who seek to stop war. A lot of us say we believe in an ideally peaceful world. The historical reality however is that this has not happened and is not happening tomorrow. An individual can change society to a degree, but the essential nature of humankind, (and the universe), cannot be changed. Scientists working on genes may say that in theory we could build a non-violent selfless person in the future. However, in reality we will probably want to build something that is more akin to a Hollywood film star, rather than seeking tolerance and love for all! What we can do as individuals and collectively is develop our self-awareness and internal happiness to a point where the problems of our own making and our own human nature can be *transcended or accepted* as part of our divine journey.

The Calmed Mind

When there is searching or seeking the journey continues. At some stage you want to be more than a searcher - and be one who has *arrived.* When you reach the right place, you don't need to go further. Enlightenment is occurring at the same time as the journey is ceasing, when all diversion and digression, and the need to block the mind stops. Simply being is a present and natural state, inherent and always active. A position where all the spiritual, religious, yogic, psychiatric, and personal growth trips and efforts are cleared. Like a breakthrough of the sun. Even if all of our life, (or lives), may seem to have no real meaning, when achieving this place, one will become truly grateful, and see all that has gone before as the work of the Divine through the human.

We don't need to become enmeshed in our own beliefs or practices from this perspective, as at the end of the day we don't need the path anymore, nor the guru, the teacher, or even a defined God. The purest elevated form of existence flows into a native state of spiritual enlightenment otherwise experienced as Existence, Knowledge, Bliss, or Sat-Chit-Ananda. This position has been known and written about over thousands of years from the time of the ancient sages and is prior to most known established religions. Nearer in history if we look closely it is expounded upon eloquently by all religions, albeit it in a variety of words, expressions and philosophy.

There are endless permutations of developed codes of religious practice, rituals and rules that are supposed to bestrew some benefit, giving a good credit rating towards the heavenly rewards. Sometimes this leads to some rejection of human natural activity such as seeking sex or wealth, even though the very acceptance of the human nature is also connected with Divine awareness. (From a Tantric perspective). In the here and now, the individual who is struggling to spiritually succeed seeks a way, which is lit up by the presence and involvement of teachers, sages or *gurus*. The true guru is the Sat (True) teacher. *Gu* means to "break through", while *Ru* means "darkness". You chose or ask for guidance on your journey, and seek it from a human teacher form, (even if not still alive). This imparter of the teaching or dispeller of darkness may just subtly project Shakti, enabling achievement of the required goal. For the spiritual seeker the guru is a grace that appears to the degree that the seeker has prepared to surrender to the guidance. It is a spark of recognition that jumps the gap between the teacher and the follower or disciple to light up the inner fires.

This following of the teacher or the guru is also part of a way, which is not about following one's basic desires, but about dealing with one's basic desires. Getting past what is binding. The characteristic behaviour or activity of an enlightened being can seem at times very ordinary or normal: a human who behaves as a human. But the path set down by the teacher endlessly addresses the problem of trying to get past or out of the human predicament, and the greed, hate, and desires that afflict us. It is then about accepting human nature and working with one's problems, continuing to practice, and not giving up on the journey in spite of lapses or even relapses from the path. There is no forceful asceticism or strident moral posturing, nor religious crusading. It is then the way of accepting the **Grace** and energy of the enlightened being and simply allowing that to promote one's own spiritual state until all the searching and seeking fall away.

Chapter 9
Looking for the Tiger

No tigers here!

I left India after ten continuous years of living there. I had not been home at all in the period & had not contacted my parents or anyone outside India. Until that is I wrote to my parents in London, and as a result received a ticket to fly Bombay to London. I returned home in 1976 having left London in 1965 at the tender age of seventeen. I went on the overland trail as a "Hippy" beatnik, smoked lots of "hashish" and spent a year getting to India. I had no income at all!

(See my book about this period: *English-Man, Beggar-Man, Holy-Man*).

My years in India were spent as a *sadhu,* a Hindu holy man, a monk, & travelling yogi. I spent several years in several different places in India. I had a first guru that I ran away from after four years never to make contact again. Later after seven years in India I met *Swami*

Muktananda in a place called *Genesh Puri*, (literally - the town of Ganesh, an Indian God). I stayed ten months in that large ashram, where Swami Muktananda had large numbers of his overseas followers. Americans, British, Australian & others were flocking to become his disciples. I stayed and had my name changed to *Ganesh Giri*, a sannyasin, (renunciate), name. However, I never took any formal initiation into the holy orders, and indeed was told that I was first and foremost an English man and would always be so. I never considered myself at the time, a full disciple of Swami Muktananda, in the mould of the rest of his Western & Indian flock. I preferred to hang around in the background and take things a bit more cautiously. I left his ashram because I wanted to see my inner guru as well as an outer one. I wanted self-realisation for myself within myself. After all that was what Swami Muktananda taught – that the guru & the Divine was within.

I spent my last three years in India living in the backwoods of Gujarat State, in a hut, thinking about little in particular, and wondering what my role in life was. I had no books or reading material or wristwatch. I just spent days & months mulling over my experiences to date with all the guru's and yogis I had met in India. I came to the conclusion eventually that I had a different type of life to experience awaiting me in England, and that the time was not yet right to plunge into a lifetime of living in India as a recluse or sannyasin.

At the age of twenty-eight, this return to my starting point in London was a big shock to my parents.

I summarise here what has been intoduces already.

I left home alone in 1965. I was seventeen and had at that time being restless to wander off and explore the world. The flames of rebellion burned within me. Rebellion from society, from parents, from the straitjacket of convention. I was not alone - the 60s were a time of foment, with the new pop culture leading, as espoused by the life, (and music of course), by the likes of the Beatles and the Rolling Stones. It was a period delineated through the birth of a youthful revolution that was to overturn the cultural norms of society at that time. The anti-establishment new generation wanted to explore new dimensions of experience, to grow long hair, wear outrageous clothes, and to experience hitherto unexplored depths of the mind with cannabis and LSD.

Influenced by my own generation I ended up on the India trail - the overland trip to Kathmandu and Nepal. I preceded a mass migration by several years, as by the time Westerners were flocking to India to guru is in large numbers, I had been ensconced there for about five years

After ten plus months on the hippy trail I reached India. The culture, like a magnet sucked me in and did not, for a while, spit me out. During my ten years continuous stay in India, I met a variety of gurus, yogis, holy men and holy women. I travelled the length of the country & at times my bed was bare concrete and my stomach was empty. Increasingly I was feted, garlanded and dined in splendour by prostrating devotees who revered all holy men, (as I had become). At the end of it all I returned to England, almost following a spur of the moment decision. I ceased overnight to speak & think and dream in Hindi. Similarly, my wraparound cloths became trousers and shirts, and I became a conventional working Englishman.

On return to England, I had little to say on the subject of my Hindu monk's life. It was a role with which I had completely identified during my stay in India, and now I was finished with it and wanted no more of it. I wanted to be the Englishman again and take on that role, but not now as a dropout hippy. I wanted to work, buy a car, drink in pubs, watch the "telly", and construct a social life for myself that was not in any way religious.

I decided on being a social worker but found that I was not wanted due to my lack of work experience. It was difficult explaining just how I passed my ten idle years in India. I found it hard once even to get a job cleaning down tables in a café! By chance or circumstances I came to apply for a position as a student psychiatric nurse.

In many ways I became the average man in the street, or the ordinary guy in the pub. I more or less forgot about my role in India to the extent even of feeling vaguely embarrassed by it all. I immigrated to New Zealand after three years and travelled around between working as a psychiatric nurse. I did think about my yoga occasionally and from time to time remembered my mantras - the sacred words that I had been initiated into in India. Occasionally I would have periods where my inner meditations would be quite profound, although externally I carried on my routine of whatever I was into that time. The spiritual side of me did pop up a few times externally. Eventually I began to think again of the spiritual aspects of my life, although I did nothing much about it until 1985. It was whilst living in Andorra that I wrote my book about my ten years in India. In 1987 I was back in New Zealand after a sojourn in various parts of Europe, (France, Monte Carlo Andorra and Spain as well as in Wales).

Then ten years had gone by in the West, in the materialistic net. I thought I was back at the beginning of a new phase that promised much more ahead. I had had ten years learning about mental illness, relationships, the way of the world, & sundry matters. I had also been lucky to have had the great fortune to experience life in some other fascinating countries & places. Now I add another thirty years plus on to this "saga". (With these writings, and perhaps more?)

The title of this part of the book: *No tigers here* - means what?

When I was a child in London I used to dream about tigers a lot, and think they were wandering outside the block of flats that I lived in. I used to read a lot of books about hunting man eating tigers and leopards and lions. After living in India, I came to believe that I'd lived there before, and that all my childhood processes had been regurgitating aspects of a previous life in India. I saw myself as having been a hunter of tigers, who then became a non-violent devotee of tigers. In dreams in India, I saw myself meeting a yogic sage outside a cave and being admonished and turned away from my hunting to become a respectful devotee of the tiger. That dream was about my previous birth: not the current one. I may have been part of the British Raj in India: possibly a collector or some official living upcountry. In India tigers were often a part of my life: certainly spiritually, as the tiger is considered to be the vehicle of the Goddess *Durga.* However, when I moved away from India I didn't think then about tigers for quite a few years. My life was not connected like it had been with India and tigers, & my worship of the Goddess. (Now I am very different, and the tiger is a core part of my life).

Finding the Tiger

In 1989 I married and over the next 30 plus years I became a family man and remain so to this time of writing. (2020). I extended my career to a satisfactory position as a senior health professional educator within mental health. I studied and received further qualifications and worked within a variety of interesting areas.

However, one key element for me over this time to the recent was my struggle to deal with a seemingly ingrained experience of *Dysthymic Depression.* (Chronic low-grade depression), with some severe episodes. I have also experienced addictive behavioural issues (dependant mostly on the depression).

> *There is a huge paradox. Now I have got to a place where I feel that I am really engaged as a spiritual soul to the maximum depth that I could ever wish, and I have found my self-realisation and my perfection (siddhi) on the spiritual plane. Yet it has come to be connected integrally with my experience of struggle with mental health.*

Interestingly I find that as I relate now to the personality that I left in India as the Hindu monk, I see that my time of ten years in India was probably about sitting in the same space where I am can sit now. (Without the need for a cave!). Also, I can look back at myself in India & make a diagnosis of depressive episodes, interspersed with the mild-to-moderate chronic depression that is called dysthymia.

*I am fascinated now by this paradoxical connection
of intense deep spiritual experience & equally
intense depression.*

This for me is *Finding the Tiger*. The tiger is my soul animal - similar to a favourite animal but not quite! The tiger represents me as being a complete whole person. Powerful in that I have my spiritual plane again, but also powerful in that I am a complete human being. I am human with my experience of the depths of despair and depression whilst at the same time have become able to deal with and cope with this part of my life. This adds to my power. I have experienced common place reality for many: the human life which can be, "weak, disabled and dysfunctional", and I am happy about this because I don't see it as bad. However, I also can be a functional health professional, family man, and "healthy human". All this alongside the choice of continuing my practice of spiritual awareness. This is about finding the Tiger: the tiger memories that drove me when I was a child to go to India, and to head off to end up as a monk. This metaphor for life has driven me now to look at the issue of spirituality and religion, and also depression in some depth.

Taming the Tiger

Not a popular path! Spiritual endeavour.

You may find few who are willing or interested in listening to your politics and religion. Your personal growth and spirituality may be in a similar vein. You then find you need to talk to specific people who are clearly interested or committed in some form of growth. Personally interested people are willing to discuss spiritual topics. However, when this topic is broached, it may be that interested parties will then talk about or even try to sell their particular brand of spirituality, which may well be connected with a specific religion. Even in company of spiritual practitioners we can find difficulties dealing with fixed rigid views, and even angrily hostile perspectives. This may be why many are put off even by the whole topic. It may seem like a can of worms.

On the whole most of society seems to be quite happy engaging in the material consumer world, except for when it bites back, and they find that suffering rather than enjoying becomes the experience. Then may arise desire for something else. The truly selfless person, the true soul seeker, does not want anything. There is a spiritual goal and transformation of purpose, but that is also selfless: it's not like a dog finding a bone and running off.

We find some of these painful experiences about life out as we go through our years. Being somewhat protected as children, we may seek again more security as we get a bit older. In our hearts we may want to develop and grow in a holistic spiritual manner and believe our path of spiritual growth will enable us to sit back in and be protected or safe. However, we may find that there are dangers in exploring and trying to move forward on a spiritual path, even though we may hold "magical thoughts" about how "wonderful" it will all be! There is even research that shows evidence of spiritual endeavour increasing mental health problems like depression. Addictions, compulsions or other psychological snakes may rear their heads, almost as if the ego fears it's "death" and wants to strike back.

Conversely it may seem that if one does all this practice with no sense of reward or desire, the goal may seem like some kind of hollow empty state - wilderness or a desert. Without actually tasting the nectar, the bliss of the Supreme Divine Grace, it is easy to feel emptiness (especially if one has given up lots of habits). Hence, we may live for a while only trusting and hoping, when we follow chosen teachings, or believe that a higher power or Divinity will "sort our lives out".

Religion can be based around desires to prosper, to flourish, to have a good place in society, or to get to heaven. We then will maintain belief & trust that God will help us to get all the things we want and help us to do the right things. The spiritual journey though, (and this is where the difference really sits), is about transcending all of this. About becoming selfless, transforming a humanness into "spiritual-ness – not saintliness". There is nothing wrong with being human wanting or achieving or seeking. Human experience itself will show the way, for when a goal is reached, this can lead to dissatisfaction and a need to go deeper. The bliss of money, food and sex will never ultimately be a permanent satisfaction or consolation. Seeking on the higher levels is where we want to have some taste of the Divine Grace nectar. We want to overcome some of the pain, sadness or general feeling of malaise about the world. We might start to feel this spiritual centre more, especially as we dig deeper into the spiritual world, and start to overhaul our materialistic striving.

Choice will always remain the individuals, and that choice will always be to go forwards or backwards or just stay in the same place. Probably not many choose to follow the path of spirituality to its deepest depths, nor would many want to become priests, monks, recluses or swamis. That however is not necessarily all of the potential "advanced" options. True "monastic" status essentially is an inner one in these modern times. Monasticism is something that was representative of spiritual or religious leaning more commonly in older times. The modern world doesn't leave much space around us to pursue that option. We have to do a lot of it on the internal plane, by making our own Divine connections and meeting in spaces where like-minded people can gather to do this work, without necessarily wearing certain clothes or performing certain rituals.

The biggest obstacle of all, is the part of us that doesn't want to die, and yet gives us most grief, and that is our ego. That is, when we seek to move into higher levels or planes the ego feels a threat, and may well set up its own conflicts and diversions to distract us for a long time. It is like a cat being removed from the warm fire to be put out into the cold – total reluctance! The human choice of life is to be very comfortable thank you very much. The way of the renunciate is not universally, commonly, or popularly cherished.

Our guides

There seems to be a series of doubts to do with how our spiritual or religious leaders have presented themselves. There are many sources of some hard questioning about gurus and spiritual teachers, now that we have the worldwide spread of the Internet. We can delve into subtle, (and not so subtle), truths about those who practice a religious or spiritual life, in the public domain.

There are questions about why many of such persons have not been able to achieve what may be considered to be, a balance, a harmony, or even sanity. Was there something intrinsically wrong with the person to start with, or did some "pollution" occur? Is it an ego somehow being bolstered up by spiritual or religious kudos and acclaim?

Even looking at older historical records of activities of great religious leaders, there have at times been things that are prompts for disgust. The modern media will spread gleefully, gory or outrageous accounts of the doings of major charismatic religious figureheads, be they of any religion. Christian pastors, Buddhist leaders and of course some really power crazed but charismatic leaders of brand-new sects, where even mass suicide has occurred. Totalitarian ministries, profligate sexual practices, or stupendous consumption of wealth is not uncommon. Where then is a serious seeker of truth to look, when seeking a path or guru?

There is instability engendered by building on one's fears and doubts, even if they have some truth, and this process should have some prominent ground in the seriously seeking enquiring mind. In all life it is best to avoid naive mistakes and blatant errors of judgement. There is also a need for some critical judgement, as to whether normal human behaviour is realistic for those with an expression of higher spiritual endeavour. Our journey is similar to a major journey or an expedition overseas. To go travelling with any company or guide, some enquiry and checks are needed. Find out about where you are going or why you want to go. Spiritual need can be at times overwhelming and propel a person directly into acting rather than thinking.

So it is probably not realistic to expect that the spiritual enlightened are all going to be fully virtuous models of society, and paragons of morals, or even nice people! It would be nice to think so, but the reality is that anyone even at the higher levels, will still be inhabiting a human body. If they are dead and long gone: E.G. Jesus or Buddha; then we are not going to get much "dirt" on them, which makes things easier. However, we may not benefit from shunning alive teachers of any description, and in fact a lot of our life is built around having teachers, so we can reap benefit in our learning journeys.

We need our many guides, and as long as we realise what we are using those guides for and avoid being sucked into some game. It is probably realistic to think that any guide that espouses higher level philosophy or spiritual practice, is only going to be relatively free of behavioural problems, addictions and negative personality traits. We do know that many in the world follow religious teachers who exhort their followers to go out and kill others, and it doesn't seem to put those followers off in the slightest. I would not see such persons as being teachers of any degree of spirituality. Religious teachers they may be, but then religion has always been associated with acts of aggression!

It seems that at some stage of the spiritual journey a conscious stock taking has to be done of all the subtle and more obvious mental, physical and emotional tendencies. Those which seem reasonably benign, (and yet set in concrete), may even be left unchanged as the spiritual goal is not human perfection, in spite of what organised religion may try to thrust upon people. The individual may choose a relatively saintly path, with or without outward display. On the other hand, the individual may simply take an, I don't care, attitude with regard to how the world responds. The spiritual journey is not about walking through a desert wilderness. There are times when there can be many temptations, as benefits may accrue from being on this journey, and temptations may be just what the ego is putting in our way to knock us back a bit.

Only at the higher stages of divine practice, and at the end of the journey does the light of perfection shine clearly.

The True Guru

"My cat is enlightened so why can't I be? Why do I still need a guru"?

Cats have it all sussed. Laze around all day in the house. No chores, no responsibilities and yet they are independent and free as they want to be. They stay out as late as they like, come and go when they please, and plenty of them have trained their owners as well, with regards to feeding times and other requirements. They are the gurus of the animal world certainly, and at times the envy of humans.

So, what's the need then to be taught better "tricks"? Why can't we just learn from nature and the people around us? Isn't a baby the best example of someone experiencing an inherently blissful natural state? Is certainly there are no shortages of learning experience on a day-to-day basis, (if we choose to accept them as such). There are people all around from whom we can learn at all times. We can also learn from our own mistakes, and from those of others. If we pursue a higher goal then there are plenty of books, and exercises to be practised, or philosophies to be pursued. In time it is quite logical, that, from the learning an individual could get a good idea of what Enlightenment, *Nirvana*, or *Moksha* is all about, and even find out how to get on the path towards such goals. (Nirvana, or Moksha are words used by Hindus or Buddhists and are Sanskrit words that describe a state of release from the cycle of birth and death, pleasure and pain).

The spiritual journey is open to anyone at any time. There are no rules which say you must have a guide, a teacher or a guru. Rather there is an understanding that all focused and energetic efforts on the spiritual journey will bring good rewards. In fact, it is logical that if you have gleaned good solid information yourself you will get better results than if you accept willy-nilly someone professing guidance, which may lead you into a mess. I am reluctant to follow recipes when cooking, as I much prefer the results, and taste, which I get from little judicious experimenting myself. The satisfaction of my own recipe gives me much more than that achieved using a textbook guide. However, in some areas, such as baking in my case, I always use a recipe!

Having a guru for the spiritual journey may even be dangerous, unless you are prepared for the acceptance of, and then proper use of, such a teacher. It's like buying a serious, expensive supercar when you are a learner driver, or when you only do a bit of city shopping by car. Or, do you plan to run a Rolls-Royce if you are employed on the "lower socio-economic scale" (i.e. poor)? Real gurus are not to be trifled with; they are for those who are willing to accept some painful truths. Also, casual acceptance of any teacher may be a gateway for further neurotic anguish rather than peace and bliss. The word guru means "one who leads from darkness to light". A guru must be already in the light to be able to reach out and help others to attain the same illumination. A guru can only affect others to the degree of that guru's own achievement.

What benefits then are to be gained by the following of an enlightened being? That teacher, that guru, may not even be alive in a physical sense. As long as the teaching remains with some system or path to be followed, then the aspirant on the spiritual journey can benefit in proportion to the efforts made. The difference with the living human guru is that a dead teacher is not going to come along with a cane to administer a rap on the knuckles. By taking on a living teacher, one is opening up to immediate evaluation, to being given marks, as in exams, and to being critically examined. The teacher is not working to allow comfort in the student. The student is not working to remain static in knowledge.

The spiritual aspirant who uses a living guru, will submit the dross, the mundane, and the un-enlightened mentality for the guru's inspection. The guru prescribes the medicine and the aspirant then moves on to the next stage - whether to take the medicine or not. The spiritual journey as gleaned from books may be quite palatable, but what the living guru may require of you personally may be "too much". This is the very reason why the true guru is necessary. If you want the spiritual journey to proceed apace, you can't stay in your comfort zone!

It's moving out of the comfort zone that is very hard, that is difficult to achieve without guidance. It is being open to inspection and evaluation that can be very uncomfortable but can be so productive. This is where the guru can work to help the spiritual aspirant. When the guru is found by a careful, even choosy search, and when the guru is approached in the appropriate manner, then the guru becomes the means for rapid progress on the spiritual journey. It is quite possible to progress spiritually by one's own efforts, and there is nothing inappropriate about this. Using the benefits of an enlightened guide however is like taking the express train rather than the slow goods train that gets "bumped off" into numerous sidings. The spiritual smorgasbord including the New Age, therapies, various sects, cults and new religions can be a temptation leading to endless side journeys, with the self-taught student ending up aimlessly sailing in a lake of spiritual hope, without getting to see the shore.

A knowledgeable guru has the present time experience of spiritual peace, awareness, and bliss that comes with real practice. This knowledgeable awareness can be "transmitted" to a student by subtle means that are not easily understood by a novice. In Sanskrit the word for this transmission is *Shakti-Paat,* the bringing down of divine Shakti energy by the guru to help awaken the natural abilities of the student, so that here and now something more concrete can be experienced regarding the nature of the spiritual goal. In Hinduism and Buddhism this energy transference is known to awaken the "third eye", or to awaken the sleeping Kundalini serpent force up through the spine. The third eye is just one way station for the chakras or centres of energy. Other areas awakened are in the heart area, the spinal centre, and also another heart "space", that is directly connected to Divine Energy.

You can choose your cat to be your guru, indeed as you can choose any person as a teacher. However, if you wanted to learn to fly jumbo jet would you take lessons from a bus driver? The importance of finding an enlightened true guru, (*Sat Guru*), may be overlooked or ignored in haste to develop one's spiritual experience within a short-term timeframe, rather than looking at the need for a long-term, solid and extensive pathway.

Chapter 10
Curing Depression with Spirituality

Depression, according to recent statistics, is practically an epidemic, with over 70 million people suffering from its effects, such as a feeling of moroseness, uselessness, lack of energy, inability to sleep, and a poor attitude toward life in general, among other symptoms. Depression causes a pessimistic view of things. It also discourages enthusiasm and stifles one's initiative. It may also produce despair and bring about sickness in the mind and body. It can make one resort to rash and thoughtless actions that a person may later regret. Much of the time, such thoughts are completely unnecessary. Thus, it is imperative that we help cure depression so that people can live with more happiness, and energy, and are thus able to reach a higher potential in life.

The reason for depression may be different for each person, and there are a variety of causes. Therefore, it must be analysed and understood. So what can we do to help cure such an attitude, as long as it is not a biological problem?

Spiritually, there are many ways to help take care of this condition. So let us take a deeper look at this.

Depression and Spirituality Components

There is often a feeling of disconnection when depressed, particularly when suicidal ideation is present. Life can feel meaninglessness, and there can be overarching wish that "I was not alive". Conversely, years ago, when I thought life was not worth living, there was in me much more devotion and prayer activity at the same time. Craving for Divinity came also, at that time, with my craving for alcohol! It was a feeling of inner emptiness, (loss of pleasure), being filled with only fear, and reactivity to life around me. I felt like an alien in this world.

There is a concept of the "sick soul", or for alcoholics it is a "spiritual disease of the soul", (as per 12-step programs). There are lots of people who feel naturally connected with the world, and they have or are born with an inner resilience which is well balanced from the outset. This speaks to the findings about inherited disorders including "addictive personalities". If one is not impulsive, and is steady on course to ones chosen career, relationships etc. then unnecessary trouble is kept at bay. On the other hand, those who are experiencing inner conflicts and/or strife in their environment will lack peace and serenity. The stage is set for mental disorders of depression/anxiety and obsessive behaviors. The original word was melancholia, as including the sense of incapacity for joyous experience. This is now one of two parts for the diagnosis of depression.

The low mood perhaps is experienced as active anguish, with a sort of psychical "deadness" not present in healthy life. Loathing, irritation and reactivity combined with fear, do not make for a happy life! Alongside is *Anhedonia,* being is the loss of enjoyment for what was previously enjoyable.

It is a dark experience, this depression. A black dog or black hole. Shame and blame then attaches itself, especially if there are episodes of substance abuse. Life can become a crisis, and the crisis mental health teams may well get involved if self-harm or suicide attempts occur.

So, what is this disharmony of the individual soul and self, and the world? Why have dark emotions and crazy impulses, and why aren't we full of positive, harmonious, and peaceful emotions?

What wrong with God's creation would say those who are skeptical about a kind and loving Creator!

My disconnection propelled me into becoming a monk in India at age eighteen. Then into a career in mental health, along with, on and off personal experiences of depression and dependency type behaviors. My quest for self-understanding, of meaning, serenity and peace led me to surrender. Suicide was potentially an option, as for a very brief period my thoughts were very dark. Now there exists a Divine Grace, which draws me out of my ego based self-personality into the light of Truth.

I worked, (as of 2025), with the depressed, the anxious, & those who have suicidal ideation. Many claim something "other" holds them back from death's door and offers hope. My depression led to disconnection with the world but not with God, and there remained an understanding inside that I would be all right. My Goddess is still with me, and I write elsewhere further of my personal pathway and belief system. (Which is more based on ancient practices from the East but includes Multi-faith components).

The disorders or mental health issues connect me to my quest, through complex interweaving of soul and Cosmic Soul, leading to my *Practical Enlightenment*. (Not just a spiritual trip, but also a space where I can realistically serve others in my *Realistic Realization* space).

Yes, my sense of healing is Goddess derived for She is my Deity. I have, however, no difficulties with other beliefs as I am Multi Faith.

Meaning can exist in the depth of dark places. The sick soul can find the healing light and receive the *Divine Grace.*

A long and painful process can be bypassed with the help of Guides and Gurus. It can be done in this life!

I saw the possibility of happiness, but it is not ordinary happiness. It is *Ananda*, the Bliss of Consciousness.

Along with spiritual consciousness as *Chit*, and spiritual Truth as *Sat.*

Sat, Chit, Ananda. The end product or desired result from the study and practice of Vedanta.

Happiness is something vastly complex, and includes the "dark forces", because it subjugates then, not eliminates them.

Evil or Satan cannot be separate from the Divine Oneness, otherwise there would not be a monotheistic God, only Duality. This is an issue or problem that Buddhism and Hinduism do not seem to have much interest in. (Even if they seem to have multiple gods). "Idol worship", does not necessarily mean that the worshiper is Dualistic in faith. It's the fundamentalists that seek to criticize other beliefs!

Natural evil is not a stumbling-block when it swallowed up in the Deity of one's choice.

Healing and harmony can take place not by denying or ignoring, but by treating professionally when indicated, whilst working to undermine the causative darkness and find a pathway that ensures a return to the Light. It is still for me about what one essentially is, a Divine Being yoked with the Cosmic Consciousness.

Fear and reactivity

What happens when all *noticeable* mental health issues are resolved, including even mild to moderate. What is left may still be negative as far as "complete" mental health goes.

Fear and Reactivity.

These two always disturb one's serenity and peace.

What can one do?

If we are embedded in our spiritual centre, we are without fear and can mix in the world at ease.

We will not accept fear and remain resistant to our reactivity.

This realized or enlightened space is a transition period even for the highly developed spiritual practitioner, because we are still in human form and still experience and display emotions. Surely, we are only talking about a small percentage that have that perfect state of realization.

The ancient sages & seers would say otherwise that we are all by nature Divine Beings, and therefore by nature can be free. Perfectly so!

Being free, means freedom from the two items of fear and resistance, but much more.

I am discussing these two in order to drill down to a sense of what this process requires.

In our claim of oneness with the Divine or Cosmic Consciousness, we have various ways of expressing the Truth of Life. In my personal philosophy, I agree with the statements espoused in Vedanta, the ancient philosophical practice from India. The core place to be as far as Vedanta is concerned is to be in awareness of Sat, Chit, Ananda. (Existence, Knowledge. Bliss). It is found in the "witness state". It is much more focused than "mindfulness".

However, this view espoused by many spiritual practitioners, is also in the domain of a variety of religious and spiritual teachers in their esoteric teachings. For instance, within the domain of Sufism or Mahayana Buddhism.

When we seek to remove the old ways through our practice, at the same time our guides, angels, or our Deity of choice moves towards us. Just as we move towards It/He/She/Them. We still get life experiences, but they are always what we need to learn through, and what we need to shine our Divinity through. We then exist in a different world, which is still the one we leave! (How does that work)?

It is all about our vibration, the expression of our soul as its enlightened self.

Therefore, we accept. We do not react. We do not fear. We deal with life and function. Then G.O.D. equals Good Orderly Direction.

As far as change goes, we accept it, but do not hasten or dramatize it. We see and probably experienced change in a much gentler fashion. However, we do not sit around saying: "*its karma, man*". Alternatively: "what will be what will be". We act and do so dynamically in times we needed to do so, when "righteous reaction" is called for. (Think of events in the Bible or the Bhagavat Gita).

We are called to transform ourselves and this world around us. We will not tolerate the darkness in all its forms. We encounter destiny as part of our realization, and that can be in the middle of a busy world, not in some cave.

We are called to serve when we accept our spiritual journey. It is not though about going out and running a soup kitchen for the homeless. That may bring us kudos in this and the afterlife and make us feel good now. True service is not motivated by ego decisions.

Growth can occur through all experience and your presence in all circumstances. Remember it is about not radiating fear or reactivity. That alone is service. Otherwise, one is just looking for the method of how to be "a good person all round".

Until this connection with the Divine occurs, the ego base self continues to look for answers through different channels. That may include therapy, treatment or medication. (Which often helps the earth-bound personality). The issue here though, is finally overcoming the confusions of self, along with the manifestations of psychological disturbance, *from its root*. This issue is about a switch to the full light of Truth, which brings release from *all darkness*.

Which brings us back to the beginning, the baseline ego based human experience of being fearful and reactive.
I have been willing to change.
The problem is, it took so long and I have gone backwards at times!

I think my Goddess understands that I have some capacity to change. It is a question of time and: "it works if you work at it". (As per A.A.)

The thing you say is "I am willing to be met and to be helped". I can do my bit it's not much". (Being humble)!

Or: "I have a devotion and I hope that due to my prayers and meditations, repetition, and devotion to my mantra, that I will be met halfway".

Met in truth.

The truth will prevail despite my efforts otherwise and despite my ego-based searching/seeking and desire for a good presentation to others.

I suppose the good thing is that I accept my personal nonsense, and I am not grabbing onto it, while seeking to have a line to the Divine Consciousness which I believe will heal me.

I am available despite my best efforts to do otherwise. I am still available for my encounter. A relationship with the Divine

If I feel I cannot understand the past, there is no point in shame or guilt. So much happens, has happened, maybe will happen? I need to align it all to my Higher Power and realise my True self.

Therefore, I threw out the rubbish, but I did not go through it to see what I was chucking out. Rubbish. Just throw it out!

I know that in my True self there is no anger, or awful reactivity, (without "righteous" full reason).
I experience folly and some frustration. (Or rather amazement about my tendency to divert from the Light).
I may have been doing my best but can be, "happily engaged", in negative thoughts behaviours and actions.
The time has come. Let us move on and be free from all the nonsense.
That is move on from the darkness to the Light, and find not only honestly, but the honesty driven by the energy that I call Divine Grace.
We can change; you can change. We can be free together.

Sex and drugs and rock 'n' roll, and more? No. I align myself to the Higher Power and yes, I still really feel the distortions of my thoughts and behaviour. (I am the "*Witness*" and am "mindful" of those thoughts).

Yet I know that my Goddess power through Divine Grace will help me and support me and guide me to the next moment. Your Deity of choice will do so also.

In that I feel free enlightened as in: "lightened from my burdens".

It is radical, this growth and ability to comprehend that there is nothing outside of the Cosmic Consciousness. True reality is there, and it's not to be thrown away, pushed away, or minimized.

However, I need to be party to doing the restorative works, which is not the same as floating on a cloud meeting a: "happy God who makes happy place".

It is about your Divinity as much as mine. In addition, it is about Divinity of the world.

My service then is this is a service to myself, and I understand if I do not do this, then this lack of intention and drive will be my depression.

So, I release all the lies and agree to allow that Grace to respond and wash over.

Accept all that has happened is years of learning, and that teachers are all people around, and all of life around.

I say yes to the Truth and now I will say I am a Divine

Being without notifying any authority to get "permission".

I can only have the awareness of my day to day, moment to moment, the best state to be in.

I do this also with my mantra yoga, which uses the names of my dancing Deity, arising up as the Kundalini energy to break through and then free from the bodily chakras.

Overcoming depression.

In spite of what you feel in depression, it may be possible to overcome depression with treatment. Then also spiritual or religious "awakenings" could be considered. It is not a matter of point of view, or mental illness beliefs. If attitude is changed dramatically then "relief" can be dramatic. This seems to occur more in the "rock bottom moments" of say, alcoholism, when relief is experience after a "religious or spiritual" experience. Mind magnifies a problem and makes it impossible to move on.

There are techniques to stop this. By not listen to the promptings of the mind. Rejecting them. Modifying them, talking back to them. (Think C.B.T & A.C.T. therapy models). In 12-step programmes it's about "stinky thinking". Participants say, "I don't go there". (Into my mind).

A cure?

Spirituality may be able to cure all forms of depression completely. It has been said as so in 12-step programmes. Although participants will also say they are in recovery "one day at a time'". Some facilities using this model do not allow residents to use medication, even if they had been on anti-depressants before entry.

Religious or spiritual conversions with total cures have happened. The odds are not great!

So, saying this, (talking about "cures"), does not seem very useful!

Will it certainly help?

Developing oneself spiritually can lay some groundwork, so you change your view about the meaning of *Life and the Universe.*

That may allow you to rise above your issues. (All of them!)

Of course, treatment options cover physical or medical factors, psychological, and spiritual factors.

In counselling we get the client to say not just what is wrong but why. Seems too basic.

Calmly thinking over things is a good start. It is also the start of Problem Solving. Do it in writing. Reflect with another person (Hopefully less depressed!). Ideally the assistance of someone you trust, who will be empathetic and non-judgemental.

Spiritually: Here add a prayer for attaining the *right help*.

Your mind is saying problems cannot be solved and overcome. The Divine within you, and the loved ones around you, can effectively solve or dissolve all your problems. Or at least help. Just do not give up.

Physical and Health Problems

Chronic physical pain often seems to go with the chronic mental pain. All aspects need to be treated.

Keep fit by participating in healthful activities. Exercise is invigorating both mentally and physically.

A good diet is very important the mind. It can be a journey in itself to find what works for you and what if any supplements have a benefit.

Yoga is useful. Just sitting in a good posture or stretching helps.

Mantras

Tap into the Divine power within and without. Use and repeat God's holy Names. Select the Mantra of choice, or better still get a mantra from a knowledgeable Guru. Repeat as much as possible.

From India we have for example the mantras:

Hari Om

Soham

Hare Krishna

Rama, Rama.

Om Namah Shivaya

And many, many more.

Also "seed" mantras associated with the chakras-described in my other books also.

Mentally repeat the mantra. (Called *japa*)

Mantra's power will then do the work for you as desired. (I.e. can be used for wealth or spiritual growth. You choose).

Mantra is vibrational healing, of the soul through to mind, body, and to your environment.

In addition, mantras create a shield of "armour" around you to protect from curses, violence and accidents. Higher vibration emanating from mantra repetition rises above darkness, or even evil forces.

It is a remedy for depression because you bypass it. It is left behind in the darkness. In the "Higher Rooms" there is only light.

You are not your body and mind. You are the "Witness" Your natural state is Sat, Chit, Ananda. Existence, Knowledge, Bliss.
Light is always you as the Divine soul. It is your birth right. You may need to connect with it., even though it is just *there*.

We separate ourselves from Light, we live in darkness. Change perspective and focus
Seek *Divine Grace*.

The Divine is perfect and complete, and emanations from the Divine, such as this world of *Life and the Universe*, are complete in purpose. Be it your belief in the Goddess as the creature, or God as Him, or as the Big Bang.

Whatever is produced in this Cosmic Consciousness is interconnected with sound.

Even though many components emanate, a wide variety of sounds are associated. A sound for each aspect. Thus, there are many mantras and each of the major ones has an extensive history of practice and is seated within a body of ancient knowledge.

Our consciousness identifies with matter, the illusion that is Maya. Matter is created and destroyed at some point of time, but nothing really disappears. Hence, we can agree with much of science here. (The Big Bang is after all a "large sound"). However, we are in fear, and rush around, because we cannot understand the essential essence of both the Transcendent self and the Maya created forms in life. We do not connect with the underlying sound. The mantra makes this connection and gives us understanding to the point of Enlightenment. After all Maya is just the Goddess going about her business!

We do not ask the real questions. Not what is your name, but what sounds are you composed of?

Our consciousness is ignored. However, we try to control nature. Unless you know yourself as Divine (in sound), all else is just fleeting experience. A trip!

Do not fear, just worry about:

Who am I?

What is reality?

What is experience?

How do I serve?

Find your mantra/s. They will attune you to the collective and the individual consciousness. Sat Chit Ananda. Mantra is a combination of special sounds and vibrations that purify space, body, mind and consciousness from negative energies. Mantra is an ancient sacred formula that gives a powerful Divine energy and is the key that opens the way to the Divine knowledge.

Repeat the mantras as much as possible any number of times.

There is manta science regarding repetition. Use a rosary or *Mala*.

108 times is considered sacred, as it is the number of Rishis, (or seers), in the sky as stars.

Chant, sing, write, or meditate silently.

The *Mala* is charging with Divine energy and thus is an excellent talisman or amulet. Treat it with due respect!

Kundalini, depression & medicine

Kundalini works in the body through the chakra centres. It flows & allows blocks to move. That is physical, psychological, mental, and emotional. Everything.

This can pay out, in the broadest sense. Hopefully, to increase Bliss. Suffering and Bliss. How these words resonate within the religious or spiritual sphere. Kundalini revealed and free to flow is synonymous with a deep spiritual awareness, and a connection with the Divine. However, at some point the full process of energy involvement through the centres or chakras becomes irrelevant. We may do our daily spiritual practice, move into the sphere of knowledge and awareness of Oneness or around us. So really the whole idea of human awakening "upwards" through the chakras can be dispense with, or reversed, as one becomes more proficient.

The same divine energy comes down to enable a somewhat different but still divine experience. From a religious perspective, we worship a divine firstly as external deity, & as a powerful being. We are at risk of being the ostrich. With head buried in the sand, if we are not aligned to divine energy presenting into our human lives, mentally and physically, *as they are.* That is the idea that meditating on kundalini arising may be somewhat misleading.

The external teacher or guru can help with clarification. Will this be Jesus, the Buddha, or our own Gurus or any source that we seek for guidance? Remember that we are already connected to the divine, because we are already part of a divine universe. This can be seen in the sense that a spark is not different in essence to the fire.

Many who write about kundalini talk of periods of despair and feelings of failure. It seems similar to reports of religious experience that at senior stage of practice, God seems to turn away. Such descriptions have a very strong correlation to that of depression as a psychiatric disorder characterized by specific symptomatology. The connection of spirituality and depression, or a deep abyss, seems there, but what about this in terms of kundalini energy? What about our own levels of enlightenment for a rising of kundalini, and does a descending of divine energy really awaken consciousness in the body?

This is in some conflict with taught aspects of our kundalini practice, but the purpose and function of kundalini is to enable us to have an experience of the witness stage, where we "see through" life *as it is*. Ultimately kundalini is a holy force aligned to the goddess energy. Otherwise known as the Holy Spirit in the West. It takes us out of our material craziness, but also it takes us through them, not passing by them or burying them. The Awakening does not make us mad or bad; we already were there!

We do however have to take what cure we really need to take and leave what we can discard. For instance, much of religion has become distorted over the years, and often serves no purpose or confuses and even destroys us. We need then to see religion as something that can help us only in parts.

Does Prozac have a place? Does Valium have a place? Do we get a therapist? Herbalist, crystal gazer, acupuncturist, psychiatrist, hypnotist. The options are multiple, but the opinions are even more so. Some believe psychiatry is the work of the Devil. For some it's the only way. In short, degrees of fundamentalism are very common. It is actually all around us in many forms and even is the new norm!

Kundalini yoga is supposed to be therapeutic. There is some research into its practice, of course quite a lot of research looks at the value of meditation. Writers in this field have express views that the kundalini process can include physical and mental problems. They also agree that the kundalini process can lead to the unveiling of the true self and enlightenment.

Depression may be located in the heart chakra; its effects appear to be in the brain area. The right side of the heart is described as a true spiritual centre. A number of teachers are very clear on this view. Depression also has echoes in monasticism and renunciation. The Sanskrit word *vairagya* means dispassion. In this case, it is almost a complete abhorrence of the world that drives a person into the state of renunciation known as *sannyas.* This seems similar to the state of *anhedonia*, which is in psychiatry is a loss of interest in all the world that previously appeared attractive.

The early life of the Buddha also illustrates this overwhelming urge through "sadness", to remove oneself from the world at all costs, even if one was a king. One view would be that he had a very low mood, the second of the two main symptoms of clinical depression. The connection between the centre of the heart and the right side of the body is an esoteric subject all of its own. The product of these two areas may be a conflict between this life of the family, society and the male female domain, and the domain of monasticism, and introspection. Its cave vs the cafe! Alternatively, we could see also a focus on good vs evil.

This primary chakra however may be more than just one chakra. It seems to be an area that is reached after the crown chakra has been breached. A sort of umbrella of light then moves down from the head to the heart area, and then all around the body.

Does the concept of depression connected to kundalini and spiritual awakening, a higher process that is trying to connect and balance both of flow and of energy to and from divine consciousness? This view meets the needs and aspirations of the human personality. In present society moving into an ever-advancing research, approaches to medical treatment to mental health may come to a recognition of kundalini type "electricity". If currently medication approaches stay limited in their effectiveness, it needs that the true workings of the brain are found, and the consequent cures thus "discovered"

Then kundalini energies may be recognized just as the power of meditation and other spiritual practice is being "discovered". At this point, we can say that psychiatric drugs to some degrees are toxins that may damage the brain, whilst healing the disorders. This is no different from saying that Panadol or aspirin is harmful. Just because we may say that psychiatry is defunct, we can also say the same about religion, or new age, or spiritual practice. In reality if we find a medication that helps us without significant side effects, there should be no conflict between our spiritual practice and scientific evidence-based medicine.

Chapter Eleven
My hut in India

Putting it into perspective.

Some autobiography here! In order to "tie together" all the previous elements & give some perspective of the "where & why of this book".

In 1973, whilst in Bombay, (now Mumbai), I was getting bored with living; in ashrams established by other people, and felt that until I had my own place, I could not get to grips with a nagging question. Was I really Ganesh Giri, a Hindu holy man, and should I settle down to a life of devotion to this role? Or was I Raymond Pattison, with a totally different lifestyle and. destiny awaiting me in England? I did not wish to give up the sadhu life if I could be a successful Hindu guru. For all my spiritual progress, I had more ego than I had possessed before I started my sadhana in India!

It is in fact well documented in yogic scriptures that when a person starts to attain any degree of progress in Sadhana, he or she can be sidetracked very easily towards social and material benefits. My desire at that stage was not so much for money, but for social power, in the form of my own band of disciples. Hindu teachings explain that according to the laws of karma*, people with great power and money have attained that position by their struggles or penances in previous lives.
*Karma - a Sanskrit word literally meaning "action".

It is that effort which produces good and bad "rewards", i.e. high and low births, heaven and hell. If the fruit of those endeavors is used wisely, then one can rise to a high level. If not used wisely, then any powers or pleasure accrued is enjoyed, and thus dissipated. This can lead to a downfall and, according to gurus I have met, this fact is illustrated in the lives of some famous, or rather infamous, people. People like Hitler, for instance, could have done some great penance in past lives, but on account of self-centered interest have been re born into a life where they have misused their karmic rewards. Once the fruit of good deeds is exhausted then a person falls from whatever high position had been achieved. The descent is usually rapid.

According to karmic philosophy, people who have done good deeds and who desire sensual pleasure will find themselves enjoying a place amongst the angels until it is time to be reborn. A spiritually minded person, however, who does good deeds and curbs the desire for rewards will not go on to heaven but will be reborn indefinitely into a suitable environment for further spiritual progress. This process continues until final and full self-realization is attained when the cycle of birth and re - birth is destroyed due to the absence of any self-centered desire.

Over the next few years, I did not attempt to change whatever destiny had been ordained by my own karma. I did not try very hard to assert myself as a guru of others and (in spite of my inner desires) and I found that I was not attracting a following of any size. Eventually I came to the conclusion that my destiny lay elsewhere, and I was even not meant to be a Hindu. Perhaps this was for the best, as my motivation contained a lot of self-interest. In the light of karmic rules, had I become at all powerful, I would have lost the benefit of my years of sacrifice and endeavor. However, I did go on to have, at least in a very small way, an ashram of my own.

I decided to move to the area of the Narmada River in Gujerat, which had been my favorite place to stay. So, I left Bombay without being fully aware of the number of months that had just passed.

I still did not have a watch, or any superfluous possessions, although I had taken to wearing footwear after six years, due to encountering the thorn strewn paths on the Narmada banks. I had ceased to wear plain drab colored ochre robes. Swami Muktananda gave me some silk dhotis and shirts in a bright orange color. 1 rather liked my new image and decided to keep this rather non ascetic look.

Apart from the "trendy" sadhu outfit though, I maintained my simple style of travel with the small shoulder bag. I never had to worry about bedding, because firstly India is usually too hot to need any, and secondly, wherever I went, I could always find a mat and a blanket if necessary. I was completely accustomed to sleeping on a hard surface with only a mat underneath, although if I stayed in someone's house, they would usually want me to have a mattress. Mosquitoes did not seem to bother me much and anyway my usual top sheet of a spare dhoti provided surprisingly good cover when stretched from toes to neck.

For a year I had found that my body had become very sensitive to the food I ate. Up until that time, I could enjoy any food that came my way, including sweets, milk, products and spicy curries. Now I found that even small quantities of tea, sugar, or chilies were giving me skin rashes. Also, if I ate any milk products or oily food, I developed indigestion and then a cold. I began to try to eat very plain fare, such plain bread and boiled vegetables without any seasoning. This was not always easy as I was often dependent on getting food as available, when given to me by a household or in an ashram. Whenever I visited a village in Gujerat I would invariably get several invitations to houses for meals. The food prepared would always be rich in spices and oils, as Gujeratis love to feed their guest the best food they can. It is, of course, a good excuse for them to have a feast too. My request for plain food would often disappoint people as they felt embarrassed to offer a sadhu guest plain roti and dhal. It also made them feel guilty if they were having "gourmet" cuisine while I dined simply. I did find, though, that people respected my ideal and need for a simple diet to a large extent, and friendly families would often go out of their way to cater for me especially.

I spent the spring and summer of 1973 wandering all over a large area to the north of the Narmada. I was getting to know a lot of people in that region, with the consequence that some "devotees" were looking around their own village localities in order to find a suitable spot for me to settle down. Many towns and villages have some sort of accommodation for passing sadhus - often a hut built next to a temple. The devout locals felt that such a facility is a necessity in accordance with their religious decrees, and hope that a yogi or mahatma of some ability will come to live in their vicinity. The devout person would then be only too happy to visit such a sadhu and make sure that all the supplies needed for his upkeep are kept flowing smoothly. There is often some competition between villages to see who can build the best temple or attract the most interesting holy man.

It is very easy to assume that the type who is always running around visiting temples and sadhus has a very simple mentality. Nothing could be further from the truth. It is the educated and the wealthy who see to the finance and upkeep of temples and ashrams. Some huge new temple complexes have been built by India's richest families, and some of the highest - placed public figures have been prominent in promoting certain gurus and sannyasin causes.

What of the poor then? Why is it that all this money is spent on temples and holy men, instead of on alleviating the misery of India's millions of destitute and poverty stricken? The Hindu philosophy or outlook on life. is that if one gives to a holy cause, i.e. a, person or place having religious merit, one accrues merit towards a place in heaven or a healthy next life. Thus, by the observance of this very fixed rule, the big temples and their priests get richer, and well-known gurus and spiritual teachers build bigger for themselves and their followers. If one gives to the poor or destitute, the gift is of limited merit! One can feed pundits and leave some scraps for the poor. One can build temples and Sanskrit colleges, leaving a few books for some local orphanage. Anything else does not result in the rewards of a wonderful after life!

After spending time in a number of small dwellings attached to little village temples, I still felt restless and undecided on the question of where to settle. My life had become a blur of places, people and events, and I was truly beginning, to tire of wandering around India. I got to the stage where I decided to stop and stay where I was, which happened to be in a village some fifty miles east of Baroda. On the outskirts of a small village in some temple grounds I had found a dilapidated hut, which was adjacent to a tiny, hardly used temple. I spent a few days as the guest of a friendly goldsmith in a nearby village.

That afternoon two men arrived to see me. They had traveled some ten miles by track, from an isolated village in an area inhabited mainly by farmers of a tribal caste. They had been sent as "envoys" to request me to come and stay in their village, which had on its outskirts a nice plot of temple land on a hill. There was a large "room" there built of mud and bricks, for the use of any sadhu who wished to stop off at the village. They said it was an ideal spot for me to stay, and I would find the outlook and tranquility most congenial. They also told me that their village was the center for a dozen surrounding satellite hamlets, and it possessed a school, a dispensary, and rudimentary shops. It also had a daily bus service (over dirt roads) to a main road, railway line, and a small town some seven miles away.

I discovered that the two men were emissaries for the group of upper caste Hindus who lived and worked in their village. This group was somewhat isolated amongst the non-vegetarian tribal castes who populated the area, lived in thatch huts and worshipped nature spirits rather than Hindu gods. Hearing somehow of my search for a place to stay, had sent me an invitation to visit them. They were also promising to look after my basic food and other needs if I decided to reside in their village.

My goldsmith host and some of his neighbors had told me that the area to which I had been invited was inhabited by semi savage people who were only on the fringe of Hinduism. Most of them neither worshipped the Hindu gods, nor were interested in sadhus and holy men. My host tried to put me off going there. However, it felt to me that destiny was calling, and I made arrangements to move to the village, which was called Kanod, later that week.

As it was the rainy season and the bus to Kanod was often suspended due to flooded roads, I had to make sure first that the way by road would be feasible. Otherwise, I would take the very muddy track route. It turned out that when the same two men from Kanod, (both farmers of the Rajput or warrior caste), came to collect me on the chosen day the bus route was open. Although Kanod was ten miles by track, taking the bus meant a trip of thirty miles and changing buses three times. However, it was much easier this way than by going on foot and crossing the innumerable muddy gullies which had become streams in the wet season.

Kanod

As we bumped along the gravel road in a dilapidated bus towards Kanod we were caught in a torrential downpour typical of the monsoon season. The skies opened up and soon we were crossing numerous streams that had sprung up instantaneously. At the approach to the village, the bus had to stop some two hundred yards short of its normal turning point just outside Kanod. A stream of some two to three feet in depth was rushing past, in what was normally a dry gully, and now formed a twenty-foot-wide watery obstacle. Everyone got off the bus and merrily formed a human chain across the turgid waters, and I was helped over the flood this way to the crowd of villagers waiting on the other side.

It turned out that I had a large welcoming party waiting to receive and garland me. Also present was a rather damp and bedraggled local band, of the village that was mostly used for wedding processions. I was ceremoniously paraded into the village to my temporary quarters. Just above the stream of water, on the village side, was a fifty-foot bank and perched above it were the temple and the "house" I would be staying in.

Several people were working there in the rain at that very moment, putting in a cement floor and generally making the place habitable for me. For the present time I was to have a room in the village hall, and there I was to spend the next week nursing a heavy cold, while the skies poured torrents outside.

Kanod was in many respects a fairly primitive backwater, but there were friendly people keen to see that I became established at the little kutir*
* Kutir - hut like dwelling, of a sadhu.

To cook on I had one slow burning primus stove. Later I built a rough outdoor fireplace where I could cook rotis and chapattis over a wood fire and thus get the best flavor in my bread. Also, I had a bed, mattress and mosquito net, although I found the area agreeably free of annoying insects.

Arrangements had been made for someone to come every morning to fetch pots of water from the nearest well some two hundred yards away down the hill, in order to give me sufficient for bathing, washing and cooking. For the equivalent of little more than a pound a month, a village girl would bring several head carried pots of water daily, as well as sweep inside and outside, and clean any dirty pots and pans. I was quite prepared to look after all my own needs, but one of the rules there was that women collect the water and do the cleaning. In my case, the village folk would have been embarrassed to see me carry my own water, and I was virtually forbidden to do so. Besides, I would be taking away a job from the poorer village girls, who did a lot of housework for wealthier households. Even an average household in India then, although incredibly poor by Western standards, could employ even poorer castes to do the cleaning, laundry and menial tasks. The richer families employ cooks, chauffeurs, night watchmen and so forth, although not usually on the scale of the British in the days of the Raj.

My role even as a poor sadhu, was definitely "upper caste" as far as the village rules and rituals were concerned and any deviation on my part would have caused offence or embarrassment. I found that even with my small "income" of donated money, I was able regularly to employ some of the village urchins to help with my garden projects. Sometimes I would employ two boys all day, when they were not at school. I paid the standard rate for adult laborers at two rupees per eight-hour day. It was half a rupee more than the child's or woman's rate. At that time there were twenty rupees to the British pound:

For many poor farmers in such villages as Kanod, supplementary paid laboring work is vital for their existence in the pre monsoon summer period. This covers the inevitable gap when their previous crop runs low or runs out altogether. Quite often I would find any work for the village boys to do in my garden, as I knew that just one rupee would buy a kilo of flour to feed their family that day. I was limited in the amount of work I could offer by my money supply, but when I received a, larger sum I employed adults to do larger scale jobs like building proper steps up to the temple.

Besides my room space, I had an outdoor verandah on one side, a tiny temple to look after, and an acre of land, including shady, bitter leaved medicinal neem trees. My plan was to develop the land into a garden with both shaded and flowery leisure areas and also to grow fruit trees and vegetables. Any villager could come and sit away from the sparse, dry landscape, which was devoid of any eye pleasing shrubbery, due to the absence of irrigation and regular rain. Many village areas in India are sparse in terms of amenities such as gardens or parks, because in poorly watered places the population spends all their lives trying to survive by growing enough food in the monsoon and winter seasons. Villages with no irrigation can be very drab and dusty places for nine months of the year. If, however, there is any spare cash in the village, it may go towards building a temple or a communal garden space just in order to provide a little color or give a shady recreational area.

I wished to make my little ashram into a well-watered haven for trees, shrubs and flowers, for all to enjoy. The trouble lay in getting water up to my area of land. I had to wait for two years until enough funds were collected to build a new well and to organize electricity and a pump. A lot of effort in the fund–raising for this enterprise was put in by one person, the village head man and doctor, who had been so instrumental initially in getting me to stay at Kanod. For two successive rainy seasons I planted a grove of trees only to see most of them wither away and die later due to the paucity of ground water from those two poor monsoons.

Many trees are planted each year in India by the forestry commissions, but if there is a poor monsoon, then a lot of their effort is wiped out. I got saplings free and often delivered, from local forestry offices, and tried hard to encourage tree planting all around the village by my own example. However, after a lot of work by my helpers, and me, the results were saddening. Not a few saplings that survived the hot summer, succumbed to the ravages of hungry and persistent cows and goats in spite of thorn barriers.

I began to see why villagers did not bother too much with planting flowers or trees in their locality. It was too difficult to keep them protected, or the rainy seasons were too sparse, or too much rain fell and flooded or washed everything away. Outside the monsoon season, the sun was merciless for the rest of the year, especially in the furnace like, shimmering heat of summer days. Even winter days were hot when the sun was up and sunbathing was unwise.

During the two thirds of the year that I was at home in Kanod, I spent much of my daytime in a state of inactivity, coming to life only in the cool of the mornings and evenings. The tin roof of my home-produced unbearable heat during the hot days, so I had constructed a tile roofed open verandah with a raised platform on the side that faced the slight breezes.

There I often sat and spent my time in a deck chair. Days, weeks, and months rushed by without really registering themselves. I had no need to clock anything or to regard time as having any influence on me. Christmas and birthdays did not exist for me, and only the big Hindu festivities brought some change into my routine. I was not bothered sitting in my deck chair or cross legged on a rug, about what was happening in the world or how my own life was passing by rapidly. I read no newspapers, I had no radio, or even time piece, and I was not interested in village gossip. I was quite content for long periods to let my *Prarabdha* take its course.

Prarabdha is a Sanskrit term frequently seen in Vedantic texts. It means literally "the fruits of previous actions". A sannyasin is not supposed to do any activity (karma), which would create fresh Prarabdha to be experienced in the next or after life. The ultimate (and proper) state for such a person is to let the fruits or consequences of previous actions, (in this or earlier lives), spend themselves naturally with the passage of time. According to Vedantic theory, Moksha or liberation from the cycle of birth and re-birth is obtained in this manner, i.e. when all Prarabdha is exhausted. Prarabdha is thus the passing of time and events that occur quite spontaneously without push or interference. To passively enjoy or suffer ones Prarabdha might seem to be an extremely negative attitude to life in terms of Western ideals and culture. In the West, the more one does or achieves (especially materially) the more one is honored or respected. In Hindu philosophy the reverse can be true (In real life this can be sometimes true). In India the person who renounces worldly striving and accomplishments is often revered by many as a holy sage, a guru, and an altogether superior type of person.

Today in the West I believe that there is a somewhat undiscovered inclination towards the ideals of Vedantic philosophy, which promotes esoteric goals. Firstly, many unemployed people, often by no choice of their own, have to come to terms with the prospect of time to spare, stretching out into the future. Secondly, people who have by self-effort obtained a large amount of leisure time for their own use are growing in numbers. The leisure orientated lifestyle is becoming a fact of western life as further automation and affluence change roles and attitudes. At the moment, most people gear their leisure time to some form of physical activity where possible. However, the advancing increase of non-working hours could create more and more space for introspection and reflective mental activity.

My stay at Kanod was marked and dominated by the vast amount of "leisure space" that I had purely to myself. As there were not many diversions to keep me busy, I found that I could sit down to think about a subject and continue my introspection in one direction for weeks on end. I did not become bored because I found even the most silent passage of time to be full of fascination. The day-to-day growth of a flower, or the scampering of a squirrel could hold my attention indefinitely. I sometimes thought that it would be interesting to be back in England, to use libraries, watch television and be "entertained" in numerous ways. When I eventually returned to England, I found that I quickly tired of the seemingly endless facilities for the occupation of leisure time. Much as children do with mud, sticks and stones, I gained more pleasure when I could occupy myself with the trivial but natural phenomena around me.

What was my mental level at that stage? Had I attained a state of self- knowledge and thus achieved Moksha? Furthermore, after all those years in India, had I found my own true religion and philosophy': If I had, did my beliefs prove to be lasting?

I developed a clearly defined philosophic outlook on life, which was not to change with the passage of time. I gained deep mental satisfaction from my knowledge of Vedanta, and I find to this day that it guides me towards calmness and equipoise, which alleviate the ups and downs of everyday life. My practice of yoga brought me to a stage where I had, if I wished, a strong degree of control over my life. For me, the sense of control over circumstances was, and is, mellowed by my acceptance by the doctrines of karma and Prarabdha, (which means some surrender to the inevitability of fate).

My resignation to the whim of destiny did at times seem to make me a pessimist. However, in the longer term I gained optimism and a belief that life events are enacted by an ordained force, which works for our ultimate benefit.

From this point of view the opposites of pain and pleasure, gain and loss, become equally acceptable. I had discovered that Mukti or Moksha is not a trance-like state but simply the ability to accept the world as it is, and ourselves as we are. This does not preclude room for change, or personal endeavor, providing, that is, that one is able to be unaffected by success or failure. Also, that any objective or goal is itself not the only end. The journey, the effort, is also a goal. In terms of self-realization, what we seek to be or achieve is already within, already available.

The Self within, the Atman of the Vedanta, is so near and yet so hard to appreciate. All the Indian yogis and Gurus that I most respect, recommend the seeker to ash the Question, "Who am I?", and also to seek the guru within as well as without. Vedantic teachers say that when we ask ourselves, "Who am I?" we are trying to find out what the true nature of the "I" is. Not the mind, not the body, but an unchanging entity that remains constant in our waking, dream and sleep states. An entity, which remains constant through childhood, adolescence, adulthood and old age. It is the Self within, the Atman, which is the same "substance" as Brahman, the Cosmic Self.

Brahman - a Sanskrit word for the impersonal "God". To be distinguished from *Brahma*, the Progenitor (one of the Vedic gods), and from a *Brahmin*, the highest caste.

I cannot define precisely what my mental state was towards the end of my stay in India. This does not matter to me. I came to realize that the mind's activities are transient and fickle, whilst the light of yogic awareness

215

burns steadily behind the mental "screens". Once having reached the transcendental inner light or awareness through our deepest subconscious, we can return to our chosen life and continue on our way bathed in a subtle serenity. My "quiet" years in an isolated Gujerati village gave me the time and space to consolidate and fortify an inner awareness.

During my stay at the small kutir in Kanod, I had few food supply problems. Often farmers would pass by my little temple after they had been out cutting by hand some crop or other. They would pop up and place a pile of wheat, rice, or pulse either in the temple or outside my door. This, plus regular donations of foodstuffs by other villagers and visitors, meant that I soon acquired stocks of grain. I had more than enough for myself and could feed any visiting sadhus or other guests. If I wished to cook, say, maize rotis, then I would fill a small tin box with maize grain and hand it, (with a small "tip"), to a village urchin for delivery to the local electric mill. In half an hour back the tin would come filled with freshly milled maize flour, warm and sweet smelling. Cooked over 'a wood fire and eaten hot such rotis of fresh flour would make a tasty meal, even on their own.

A lot of the grain I used had been grown in fields fertilized by natural manure (as the farmers could afford no other). Such grain produced much sweeter and tastier flour than the artificially fertilized version. In today's world of so-called "gourmet" foods, it is a pity that the real taste of naturally grown produce is experienced by few.

Almost daily during the cooler times of the day, I walked out into the surrounding area of field, scrub and gullies. during the season when crops were ripening, I would often be invited into someone's field to sample the produce. I had freshly picked corn on the cob roasted over twigs, or peanuts straight from the ground toasted in a similar fashion. Several farmers invited me to collect and pick green peas and pulses whenever needed for my pot. Vegetables were rarely grown by locals, even in the rainy season with the exception of chilies. Occasionally someone grew a few onions and perhaps potatoes or eggplants. Most villagers in this area, with the exception of the higher castes, rarely ate any vegetable dishes other than potatoes curried with fresh green or red chilies. In fact, the average villager's vitamin intake seemed to be derived purely from the large quantities of hot peppers consumed, often ground up as a chutney. Frequently this was the only accompaniment to a. roti meal in a poor household, where dhal and other "necessities" were unaffordable luxuries on many days of the year.

I managed to grow a lot of vegetables in the rainy season, and planted peas, marrows and courgettes. In the summer I made use of lemons, which grew abundantly. Otherwise, my vitamin intake was limited and irregular, especially as I could not eat chilies.

My body reacted to anything other than plain food, and in order to find out exactly how various foods affected me I experimented with a variety of diets. The diet that kept me in best health, I found, was a sparse regime of grains, pulses and vegetables - excluding salt, spices, sugar, tea, and all fatty products. I discovered that, perhaps due to the hot climate's effect and my lazy lifestyle, I could not happily digest oily food or milk products. At one point, for a month or so, I tried a diet of only fresh, hot rotis - with absolutely no other intake except water. This very plain regime of bread and water solely, did me no harm at all, and I even enjoyed the experience. In fact, I found that by having no variety of taste in my food, I was able (after a while) to derive just as much overall taste satisfaction from plain bread as from a varied diet.

I did not fully know then why I was so sensitive to so many food items. My weight since my arrival in India had been a very low 130 lbs., in spite of trying at previous times to put on pounds with rich foods. Also, I always ate large quantities of carbohydrates even when I was on my simple diet. I feel that the large amounts of grain foods that I ate played a significant part in my skinniness, along with the debilitating effect of the intense heat. For slimmer's I can recommend eating as much as you like providing you avoid sugar, processed white grain, and all products containing fat or oil. Whole wheat and nonfat pulse proteins help to produce a digestive fire within the body, akin to fueling a fire with dry twigs. Thus, the appetite and the digestive powers are increased and yet the body remains slim.

It is very difficult in India to avoid getting the occasional bout of a fairly serious illness. At Kanod I had a few alarming fevers. I hated taking antibiotics and during one bout of fever I became seriously ill and had an extremely high temperature. The village doctor persuaded me to take some Chloromycetin, and I duly recovered after a week or so. Afterwards I was told that probably I had suffered an attack of typhoid fever, and I could have died.

There are all sorts of illnesses and hazards to be found in India, all waiting to kill one off very quickly. My destiny, however, was to come through, at least that period in India, unscathed. Villagers succumbed to illnesses like tetanus, usually after cutting themselves with a farm implement and then not seeking medical help. Rabies was another hazard. The towns and villages were full of mangy stray dogs, which were a health risk apart from their bites. Bites from another common creature, the snake, were an ever-present risk for the worker cutting crops by hand, especially as the time spent getting to the nearest medical help often meant certain death. A Kanod man got bitten on the head whilst carrying a bale of freshly cut grass. The snake had slithered into the bale somehow and bit the farmer as he was carrying it in the normal Indian fashion. He survived due to the immediate medical attention, and serum, he received at the Kanod dispensary.

I saw snakes around Kanod from time to time and some of them were huge. I glimpsed one sliding through the center of a large bush. It was as thick as an arm and its body just kept sliding endlessly past. I never got to see its tail or head as I moved away pretty quickly. It was only on a few occasions that I saw snakes around my kutir as I used to have a number of mongooses in nearby residence. I found a deadly poisonous snake in my room one day, but it left without much persuasion by prodding with a long stick. My main problem, especially in the monsoon season, was scorpions. They tended to scuttle around when the air was warm and humid, particularly at night. When I sat outside on such evenings or meditated in the dark, I always shone a torch around and looked carefully where I put my feet. Though not necessarily fatal, the scorpion sting gives a nasty jolt to the heart and produces much pain and swelling to follow. I once got stung on the finger by a baby one that was hidden in a piece of moldy wood, which I had picked up for the fire. Its sting was like a large jolt of high voltage electricity shooting up my arm to my heart. Luckily little poison entered my finger, and I suffered briefly and mildly.

Scorpions carry their poisons in a little sac at the end of their tail. A needle like barb protrudes from the sac and is used for injecting the "victim". If I found a scorpion in my room, I would pick it up by the tail with the long tongs that I used for handling embers of the fire. Some kids from the village used to dig out scorpions from their holes in earth banks and catch them by the tail with something suitable. Then they would cut off the poisonous sac, tie a string to the tail, and parade their newfound "pets" around for a while until the novelty wore off.

I had a variety of animals dwelling in and around my acre plot. Squirrels nested between the walls and the roof of my kutir where there was quite a wide channel along the double thickness of the bricks. I could not see the channel, but I could hear animals using it. Occasionally a baby squirrel would fall down from a hole in one corner into my room. The mother would then poke her head out and start squeaking frantically while the baby stumbled around. The fall did not seem to do them any harm as even the smallest squirrel seems adept at landing upright and safe after a long drop. I used to grab the baby ones in a cloth and return them, squealing, to their home. I found out quite quickly that a thick cloth was necessary as even tiny squirrels have very sharp teeth. Rats were more unwelcome visitors, and they also used the gap under the roof as a home at various times. They then scrambled down my walls at night to get at my food stores. I used to trap them and then release them a long way away in the fields. One other strange creature that took up residence was a giant armored lizard that looked like a small crocodile. I saw it once or twice in the evening on its way out to the fields. It was apparently a rare, shy creature that usually kept well away from human habitations. Less shy were the lizards that clung motionless to my inner wall during the day. They moved around at night and kept the place free of cockroaches. If they saw one, they would pounce at great speed and gobble up their giant meal with a loud crunching noise.

I was able to spend many hours observing the animals and birds around me, and also watch my flowers, saplings and plants grow (or wither) day by day. Nowadays I do not always notice the flora and fauna around me. It was only when I had endless time to sit and watch that I was really aware of nature's variety. In my home at Kanod the squirrels, the lizards, and even the rats were part of the animal family of my little temple area, and I was always aware of any changes in the wildlife of my garden.

In the very hot summer weather, I took to sleeping outside where a mild breeze made the nights bearably cool. I had my bed above the ground of course, but I found that I slept very lightly, perhaps like an animal does, with some senses on guard. I felt that part of me was always awake, listening out for any untoward sounds. I can understand how an animal in the jungle feels, unable to relax like humans do in their secure houses. I was never too worried, however, about being on my own at night, in a corner of the fields without recourse to quick assistance in case of trouble. I had to accept and believe that the world around me was basically my nurturer and not my enemy.

This attitude I have found to be of immense benefit, not just in "wild" places, but also in everyday life. After all, the modern world is itself a dense jungle - which harbors its own multitude of deadly perils, as well as being the provider of innumerable benefits.

Goodbye India

After nearly three years at Kanod I began to think that perhaps I was destined to spend the rest of my life in India. I thought deeply about making an effort to establish some sort of ashram or haven out of my humble surroundings. I wanted more than the simplicity around me, and I hankered after developing the place into something that was, frankly, materialistic in many respects. It took me a while to arrive at the very obvious, logical conclusion that I was not really happy with my simple Indian life, because I still aspired to the "affluence" that I knew I could have in England. After a while, I began to recognize again that my destiny was not, perhaps, after all the sadhu life, either spent in my little kutir or in wandering around India.

However, I travelled a lot to near and distant villages or towns to which I had been invited by a variety of "devotees". I gave a few talks or lectures here and there and was starting to be the guru of a number of families spread over a wide area of Gujerat. I knew that if I was patient and built up my following over say ten years, then I could develop my base into an ashram that resembled something like that of my ambitions. However, quite suddenly the whole idea of staying in India started to seem rather strange and unnatural for me.

In a most intriguing way, I began to dream and think of England and. English things regularly. This was the re-awakening of an area of my mind that had seemed extinct. I started to think in English again, rather than in Hindi or the Gujerati in which I was becoming proficient. I began to appreciate speaking English when I met those who spoke it well, and started to seek out news of world events, and to read books on non-religious subjects. I began even to think of my parents for the first time in eight or nine years. I had a peculiar feeling as if a veil had suddenly been lifted, allowing my previous identity as Raymond to intermingle with my Indian role as Ganesh Giri. I sensed that my life in India was reaching the point of maturity, and that I could achieve no more in my endeavors to fathom the depths of Hinduism and yogic lore. I did not feel that I had achieved the perfection of my sadhu lifestyle, but then I no longer needed such a goal. Something was pulling me in a radical new direction, not for the first time in my life.

Paramhansa Swami Ganeshi Giri

1975 Gujerat India

Paramhansa Swami Ganeshi Giri

(Procession held by villagers)

Moving into residence at Kanod village

1973 Gujerat India

About Raymond

In my younger years, from 1976, I was a monk in India for 10 years. (*Ganesh Giri Paramhansa*). Four books written to 2022. *I write & talk about Yoga, Mantras, Kundalini, and Gurus.*

Author Pages:

https://www.amazon.com/author/om-divine-grace-mantra-yoga

I have been a Mental Health Practitioner since 1980.

Get Mantra information & more on my web/blog site: www.goddessmantra.guru

Also Om Divine Grace podcasts/ Mantra Guru-Raymond YouTube – for Kundalini tutorials.

I believe that Divine Grace has got me where I am, & now guides me, & inspires the writing. I share my experience & knowledge as a service, whilst respecting others beliefs, & what may work best

My books are in paperback & eBooks:

English-Man, Beggar-Man, Holy-Man

My journey overland to India in 1976, & my 10 years there a monk

Goddess Inspired - Collected Writings

The Transcendental Guru - (By Paramhansa Ganesh Giri)

Om Divine Grace Yoga - (By Paramhansa Ganesh Giri)

MY MANTRA ART: https://fineartamerica.com/art/raymond+pattison

Mantra for Enlightenment from: mantraguru.raymond@gmail.com

Made in the USA
Monee, IL
07 July 2026